I0016527

FORWARD/COMMENTARY

The National Institute of Standards and Technology (NIST) is a measurement standards laboratory, and a non-regulatory agency of the United States Department of Commerce. Its mission is to promote innovation and industrial competitiveness. Founded in 1901, as the National Bureau of Standards, NIST was formed with the mandate to provide standard weights and measures, and to serve as the national physical laboratory for the United States. With a world-class measurement and testing laboratory encompassing a wide range of areas of computer science, mathematics, statistics, and systems engineering, NIST's cybersecurity program supports its overall mission to promote U.S. innovation and industrial competitiveness by advancing measurement science, standards, and related technology through research and development in ways that enhance economic security and improve our quality of life.

The need for cybersecurity standards and best practices that address interoperability, usability and privacy has been shown to be critical for the nation. NIST's cybersecurity programs seek to enable greater development and application of practical, innovative security technologies and methodologies that enhance the country's ability to address current and future computer and information security challenges.

The cybersecurity publications produced by NIST cover a wide range of cybersecurity concepts that are carefully designed to work together to produce a holistic approach to cybersecurity primarily for government agencies and constitute the best practices used by industry. This holistic strategy to cybersecurity covers the gamut of security subjects from development of secure encryption standards for communication and storage of information while at rest to how best to recover from a cyber-attack.

The field of computer science is rapidly changing from the basic personal computer to the "Internet of Things". Many of these devices were not designed to be "connected" and very little thought was given to secure them from cyber-attack. Recent events have clearly demonstrated the need to secure everything from web cams to electrical utility grids.

That's where NIST comes in. Just as the National Bureau of Standards set the standard for weights and measures at the beginning of the last century, the 21st century mission for NIST is to set the standard for cybersecurity. NIST gathers the very best minds in industry and government and serves as the central clearing house for information that sets the standard for security for the nation. This publication is only one piece in the mosaic of publications NIST produces but each is a vital key in its own field to the overall cybersecurity strategy that government and industry must adopt in the public interest. All NIST publications are freely available for download over the internet to maximize adoption of the standards.

This NIST Special Publication is an integral part of the overall design, development and maintenance of an IT security infrastructure that ensures confidentiality, integrity, and availability of mission critical information. It was developed to assist in choosing IT security products that meet an organization's requirements. It should be used with other NIST publications to develop a comprehensive approach to managing, satisfying, and verifying an organization's IT security and information assurance requirements.

We here at 4th Watch Books are former government employees so we know how government employees actually use the standards. When a new standard is released, an engineer prints it out, punches holes and puts it in a 3-ring binder. While this is not a big deal for a 5 or 10-page document, many NIST documents are over 100 pages and printing a large document is a time-consuming effort. Unfortunately, reductions in government over the years means that now the engineer himself has to print his own copy (no one has a secretary anymore). So, an engineer that's paid $75 an hour is spending hours simply printing out the tools he needs to do his job. That's time that could be better spent doing engineering.

4th Watch Books prints these documents so engineers can focus on what they were hired to do – engineering. This is important because there are not as many engineers working in government as there used to be, so wasted time on clerical duties is unproductive. As a former senior leader in the government, I always encouraged my subordinates to look for ways to do things better, faster, cheaper. I always asked my staff to focus on the objective and consider the cost/benefit analysis of everything they do. If something can be done better, faster and cheaper, then we would be remiss if we didn't take advantage of the opportunity.

This book is a perfect example of that type of thinking. Rather than spend the limited resources we have at a particular agency to develop cybersecurity solutions, it will always be better, faster and cheaper to embrace a standard that has been fully-developed and totally integrated in the wider scheme of things by the engineers at NIST with the help they receive from industry.

Luis Ayala
Writer and Publisher, 4th Watch Books

Mr. Ayala began his career in 1970 when he was drafted during the Vietnam Police Action and served 4 years in the U.S. Air Force, Strategic Air Command. With 40+ years of experience, he has led multi-million dollar federal programs for USACE, NAVFAC, GSA, and the Intelligence Community. He is a former Senior Technical Expert at the Defense Intelligence Agency with in-depth technical experience. He is an avid writer on the subject of the threats of cyber-physical attacks on America.

Copyright © 2017 Luis Ayala All rights reserved

National Institute of Standards and Technology

U.S. Department of Commerce

Special Publication 800-115

Technical Guide to Information Security Testing and Assessment

Recommendations of the National Institute of Standards and Technology

Karen Scarfone
Murugiah Souppaya
Amanda Cody
Angela Orebaugh

NIST Special Publication 800-115

Technical Guide to Information Security Testing and Assessment

Recommendations of the National Institute of Standards and Technology

Karen Scarfone
Murugiah Souppaya
Amanda Cody
Angela Orebaugh

COMPUTER SECURITY

Computer Security Division
Information Technology Laboratory
National Institute of Standards and Technology
Gaithersburg, MD 20899-8930

September 2008

U.S. Department of Commerce

Carlos M. Gutierrez, Secretary

National Institute of Standards and Technology

Dr. Patrick D. Gallagher, Deputy Director

Reports on Computer Systems Technology

The Information Technology Laboratory (ITL) at the National Institute of Standards and Technology (NIST) promotes the U.S. economy and public welfare by providing technical leadership for the nation's measurement and standards infrastructure. ITL develops tests, test methods, reference data, proof of concept implementations, and technical analysis to advance the development and productive use of information technology (IT). ITL's responsibilities include the development of technical, physical, administrative, and management standards and guidelines for the cost-effective security and privacy of sensitive unclassified information in Federal computer systems. This Special Publication 800-series reports on ITL's research, guidance, and outreach efforts in computer security and its collaborative activities with industry, government, and academic organizations.

National Institute of Standards and Technology Special Publication 800-115
Natl. Inst. Stand. Technol. Spec. Publ. 800-115, 80 pages (Sep. 2008)

Certain commercial entities, equipment, or materials may be identified in this document in order to describe an experimental procedure or concept adequately. Such identification is not intended to imply recommendation or endorsement by the National Institute of Standards and Technology, nor is it intended to imply that the entities, materials, or equipment are necessarily the best available for the purpose.

Acknowledgements

The authors, Karen Scarfone and Murugiah Souppaya of the National Institute of Standards and Technology (NIST) and Amanda Cody and Angela Orebaugh of Booz Allen Hamilton, wish to thank their colleagues who reviewed drafts of this document and contributed to its technical content. The authors would like to acknowledge John Connor, Tim Grance, Blair Heiserman, Arnold Johnson, Richard Kissel, Ron Ross, Matt Scholl, and Pat Toth of NIST and Steve Allison, Derrick Dicoi, Daniel Owens, Victoria Thompson, Selena Tonti, Theodore Winograd, and Gregg Zepp of Booz Allen Hamilton for their keen and insightful assistance throughout the development of the document. The authors appreciate all the feedback provided during the public comment period, especially by Marshall Abrams, Karen Quigg, and others from MITRE Corporation; William Mills of SphereCom Enterprises; and representatives from the Financial Management Service (Department of the Treasury) and the Department of Health and Human Services (HHS).

Trademark Information

All names are registered trademarks or trademarks of their respective companies.

Table of Contents

Executive Summary ES-1

1. Introduction 1-1
   1.1 Authority 1-1
   1.2 Purpose and Scope 1-1
   1.3 Audience 1-1
   1.4 Document Structure 1-2

2. Security Testing and Examination Overview 2-1
   2.1 Information Security Assessment Methodology 2-1
   2.2 Technical Assessment Techniques 2-2
   2.3 Comparing Tests and Examinations 2-3
   2.4 Testing Viewpoints 2-4
       2.4.1 External and Internal 2-4
       2.4.2 Overt and Covert 2-5

3. Review Techniques 3-1
   3.1 Documentation Review 3-1
   3.2 Log Review 3-1
   3.3 Ruleset Review 3-2
   3.4 System Configuration Review 3-3
   3.5 Network Sniffing 3-4
   3.6 File Integrity Checking 3-4
   3.7 Summary 3-5

4. Target Identification and Analysis Techniques 4-1
   4.1 Network Discovery 4-1
   4.2 Network Port and Service Identification 4-3
   4.3 Vulnerability Scanning 4-4
   4.4 Wireless Scanning 4-6
       4.4.1 Passive Wireless Scanning 4-8
       4.4.2 Active Wireless Scanning 4-9
       4.4.3 Wireless Device Location Tracking 4-9
       4.4.4 Bluetooth Scanning 4-10
   4.5 Summary 4-10

5. Target Vulnerability Validation Techniques 5-1
   5.1 Password Cracking 5-1
   5.2 Penetration Testing 5-2
       5.2.1 Penetration Testing Phases 5-2
       5.2.2 Penetration Testing Logistics 5-5
   5.3 Social Engineering 5-6
   5.4 Summary 5-7

6. Security Assessment Planning 6-1
   6.1 Developing a Security Assessment Policy 6-1
   6.2 Prioritizing and Scheduling Assessments 6-1
   6.3 Selecting and Customizing Techniques 6-3

6.4 Assessment Logistics 6-4
    6.4.1 Assessor Selection and Skills...6-5
    6.4.2 Location Selection 6-6
    6.4.3 Technical Tools and Resources Selection 6-8
6.5 Assessment Plan Development 6-10
6.6 Legal Considerations 6-12
6.7 Summary 6-12

7. Security Assessment Execution...**7-1**

7.1 Coordination...7-1
7.2 Assessing...7-2
7.3 Analysis..7-3
7.4 Data Handling 7-4
    7.4.1 Data Collection 7-5
    7.4.2 Data Storage 7-5
    7.4.3 Data Transmission..7-6
    7.4.4 Data Destruction...7-7

8. Post-Testing Activities **8-1**

8.1 Mitigation Recommendations..8-1
8.2 Reporting 8-1
8.3 Remediation/Mitigation 8-2

List of Appendices

Appendix A— Live CD Distributions for Security Testing **A-1**

Appendix B— Rules of Engagement Template...**B-1**

Appendix C— Application Security Testing and Examination **C-1**

Appendix D— Remote Access Testing...**D-1**

Appendix E— Resources **E-1**

Appendix F— Glossary **F-1**

Appendix G— Acronyms and Abbreviations **G-1**

List of Tables

Table 3-1. Review Techniques 3-5

Table 3-2. Baseline Skill Set for Review Techniques 3-5

Table 4-1. Target Identification and Analysis Techniques 4-10

Table 4-2. Baseline Skill Set for Target Identification and Analysis Techniques ...4-11

Table 5-1. Target Vulnerability Validation Techniques 5-7

Table 5-2. Security Testing Knowledge, Skills, and Abilities 5-7

Table A-1. BackTrack Toolkit Sample A-1

Table A-2. Knoppix STD Toolkit Sample A-2

Table E-1. Related NIST Documents E-1

Table E-2. Online Resources E-1

List of Figures

Figure 5-1. Four-Stage Penetration Testing Methodology 5-3

Figure 5-2. Attack Phase Steps with Loopback to Discovery Phase 5-4

Executive Summary

An information security *assessment* is the process of determining how effectively an entity being assessed (e.g., host, system, network, procedure, person—known as the assessment *object*) meets specific security objectives. Three types of assessment methods can be used to accomplish this—testing, examination, and interviewing. *Testing* is the process of exercising one or more assessment objects under specified conditions to compare actual and expected behaviors. *Examination* is the process of checking, inspecting, reviewing, observing, studying, or analyzing one or more assessment objects to facilitate understanding, achieve clarification, or obtain evidence. *Interviewing* is the process of conducting discussions with individuals or groups within an organization to facilitate understanding, achieve clarification, or identify the location of evidence. Assessment results are used to support the determination of security control effectiveness over time.

This document is a guide to the basic technical aspects of conducting information security assessments. It presents technical testing and examination methods and techniques that an organization might use as part of an assessment, and offers insights to assessors on their execution and the potential impact they may have on systems and networks. For an assessment to be successful and have a positive impact on the security posture of a system (and ultimately the entire organization), elements beyond the execution of testing and examination must support the technical process. Suggestions for these activities—including a robust planning process, root cause analysis, and tailored reporting—are also presented in this guide.

The processes and technical guidance presented in this document enable organizations to:

- Develop information security assessment policy, methodology, and individual roles and responsibilities related to the technical aspects of assessment

- Accurately plan for a technical information security assessment by providing guidance on determining which systems to assess and the approach for assessment, addressing logistical considerations, developing an assessment plan, and ensuring legal and policy considerations are addressed

- Safely and effectively execute a technical information security assessment using the presented methods and techniques, and respond to any incidents that may occur during the assessment

- Appropriately handle technical data (collection, storage, transmission, and destruction) throughout the assessment process

- Conduct analysis and reporting to translate technical findings into risk mitigation actions that will improve the organization's security posture.

The information presented in this publication is intended to be used for a variety of assessment purposes. For example, some assessments focus on verifying that a particular security control (or controls) meets requirements, while others are intended to identify, validate, and assess a system's exploitable security weaknesses. Assessments are also performed to increase an organization's ability to maintain a proactive computer network defense. Assessments are not meant to take the place of implementing security controls and maintaining system security.

To accomplish technical security assessments and ensure that technical security testing and examinations provide maximum value, NIST recommends that organizations:

- **Establish an information security assessment policy.** This identifies the organization's requirements for executing assessments, and provides accountability for the appropriate individuals to ensure assessments are conducted in accordance with these requirements. Topics that an assessment policy should address include the organizational requirements with which assessments must comply, roles and responsibilities, adherence to an established assessment methodology, assessment frequency, and documentation requirements.

■ **Implement a repeatable and documented assessment methodology.** This provides consistency and structure to assessments, expedites the transition of new assessment staff, and addresses resource constraints associated with assessments. Using such a methodology enables organizations to maximize the value of assessments while minimizing possible risks introduced by certain technical assessment techniques. These risks can range from not gathering sufficient information on the organization's security posture for fear of impacting system functionality to affecting the system or network availability by executing techniques without the proper safeguards in place. Processes that minimize risk caused by certain assessment techniques include using skilled assessors, developing comprehensive assessment plans, logging assessor activities, performing testing off-hours, and conducting tests on duplicates of production systems (e.g., development systems). Organizations need to determine the level of risk they are willing to accept for each assessment, and tailor their approaches accordingly.

■ **Determine the objectives of each security assessment, and tailor the approach accordingly.** Security assessments have specific objectives, acceptable levels of risk, and available resources. Because no individual technique provides a comprehensive picture of an organization's security when executed alone, organizations should use a combination of techniques. This also helps organizations to limit risk and resource usage.

■ **Analyze findings, and develop risk mitigation techniques to address weaknesses.** To ensure that security assessments provide their ultimate value, organizations should conduct root cause analysis upon completion of an assessment to enable the translation of findings into actionable mitigation techniques. These results may indicate that organizations should address not only technical weaknesses, but weaknesses in organizational processes and procedures as well.

1. Introduction

1.1 Authority

The National Institute of Standards and Technology (NIST) developed this document in furtherance of its statutory responsibilities under the Federal Information Security Management Act (FISMA) of 2002, Public Law 107-347.

NIST is responsible for developing standards and guidelines, including minimum requirements, for providing adequate information security for all agency operations and assets; but such standards and guidelines shall not apply to national security systems. This guideline is consistent with the requirements of the Office of Management and Budget (OMB) Circular A-130, Section 8b (3), "Securing Agency Information Systems," as analyzed in A-130, Appendix IV: Analysis of Key Sections. Supplemental information is provided in A-130, Appendix III.

This guideline has been prepared for use by federal agencies. It may be used by nongovernmental organizations on a voluntary basis and is not subject to copyright, though attribution is desired.

Nothing in this document should be taken to contradict standards and guidelines made mandatory and binding on federal agencies by the Secretary of Commerce under statutory authority; nor should these guidelines be interpreted as altering or superseding the existing authorities of the Secretary of Commerce, Director of the OMB, or any other federal official.

1.2 Purpose and Scope

The purpose of this document is to provide guidelines for organizations on planning and conducting technical information security testing and assessments, analyzing findings, and developing mitigation strategies. It provides practical recommendations for designing, implementing, and maintaining technical information relating to security testing and assessment processes and procedures, which can be used for several purposes—such as finding vulnerabilities in a system or network and verifying compliance with a policy or other requirements. This guide is not intended to present a comprehensive information security testing or assessment program, but rather an overview of the key elements of technical security testing and assessment with emphasis on specific techniques, their benefits and limitations, and recommendations for their use.

This document replaces NIST Special Publication 800-42, *Guideline on Network Security Testing*.

1.3 Audience

This guide is intended for use by computer security staff and program managers, system and network administrators, and other technical staff who are responsible for the technical aspects of preparing, operating, and securing systems and network infrastructures. Managers can also use the information presented to facilitate the technical decision-making processes associated with security testing and assessments. Material in this document is technically oriented, and assumes that readers have at least a basic understanding of system and network security.

1.4 Document Structure

The remainder of this document is organized into seven major sections:

- Section 2 presents an overview of information security assessments, including policies, roles and responsibilities, methodologies, and techniques.

- Section 3 provides a detailed description of several technical examination techniques, including documentation review, log review, network sniffing, and file integrity checking.

- Section 4 describes several techniques for identifying targets and analyzing them for potential vulnerabilities. Examples of these techniques include network discovery and vulnerability scanning.

- Section 5 explains techniques commonly used to validate the existence of vulnerabilities, such as password cracking and penetration testing.

- Section 6 presents an approach and process for planning a security assessment.

- Section 7 discusses factors that are key to the execution of security assessments, including coordination, the assessment itself, analysis, and data handling.

- Section 8 presents an approach for reporting assessment findings, and provides an overview of remediation activities.

This guide also contains the following appendices:

- Appendix A describes two live operating system (OS) CD distributions that allow the user to boot a computer to a CD containing a fully operational OS and testing tools.

- Appendix B provides a template for creating Rules of Engagement (ROE).

- Appendix C briefly discusses application security assessment.

- Appendix D contains recommendations for performing remote access testing.

- Appendix E offers a list of resources that may facilitate the security assessment process.

- Appendix F features a glossary of terms used throughout this document.

- Appendix G provides a list of acronyms and abbreviations.

2.   Security Testing and Examination Overview

An information security *assessment* is the process of determining how effectively an entity being assessed (e.g., host, system, network, procedure, person—known as the assessment *object*) meets specific security objectives. Three types of assessment methods can be used to accomplish this—testing, examination, and interviewing. *Testing* is the process of exercising one or more assessment objects under specified conditions to compare actual and expected behaviors. *Examination* is the process of checking, inspecting, reviewing, observing, studying, or analyzing one or more assessment objects to facilitate understanding, achieve clarification, or obtain evidence. *Interviewing* is the process of conducting discussions with individuals or groups within an organization to facilitate understanding, achieve clarification, or identify the location of evidence. Assessment results are used to support the determination of security control effectiveness over time.

This publication addresses technical testing and examination techniques that can be used to identify, validate, and assess technical vulnerabilities and assist organizations in understanding and improving the security posture of their systems and networks. Security testing and examination is required by FISMA[1] and other regulations. It is not meant to take the place of implementing security controls and maintaining system security, but to help organizations confirm that their systems are properly secured and identify any organization security requirements that are not met as well as other security weaknesses that should be addressed.

This section provides an overview of information security assessment methodologies and technical testing and examination techniques.

2.1   Information Security Assessment Methodology

A repeatable and documented security assessment methodology is beneficial in that it can:

- Provide consistency and structure to security testing, which can minimize testing risks

- Expedite the transition of new assessment staff

- Address resource constraints associated with security assessments.

Because information security assessment requires resources such as time, staff, hardware, and software, resource availability is often a limiting factor in the type and frequency of security assessments. Evaluating the types of security tests and examinations the organization will execute, developing an appropriate methodology, identifying the resources required, and structuring the assessment process to support expected requirements can mitigate the resource challenge. This gives the organization the ability to reuse pre-established resources such as trained staff and standardized testing platforms; decreases time required to conduct the assessment and the need to purchase testing equipment and software; and reduces overall assessment costs.

A phased information security assessment methodology offers a number of advantages. The structure is easy to follow, and provides natural breaking points for staff transition. Its methodology should contain at minimum the following phases:

---

[1]   Section 3544 requires the "periodic testing and evaluation of the effectiveness of information security policies, procedures, and practices, to be performed with a frequency depending on risk, but no less than annually." FISMA is available at http://csrc.nist.gov/drivers/documents/FISMA-final.pdf.

- **Planning**. Critical to a successful security assessment, the planning phase is used to gather information needed for assessment execution—such as the assets to be assessed, the threats of interest against the assets, and the security controls to be used to mitigate those threats—and to develop the assessment approach. A security assessment should be treated as any other project, with a project management plan to address goals and objectives, scope, requirements, team roles and responsibilities, limitations, success factors, assumptions, resources, timeline, and deliverables. Section 6 of this guide covers planning.

- **Execution**. Primary goals for the execution phase are to identify vulnerabilities and validate them when appropriate. This phase should address activities associated with the intended assessment method and technique. Although specific activities for this phase differ by assessment type, upon completion of this phase assessors will have identified system, network, and organizational process vulnerabilities. This phase is discussed in more depth in Section 7.

- **Post-Execution**. The post-execution phase focuses on analyzing identified vulnerabilities to determine root causes, establish mitigation recommendations, and develop a final report. Section 8 of this guide addresses reporting and mitigation.

Several accepted methodologies exist for conducting different types of information security assessments. References to several of these methodologies are found in Appendix E.[2] For example, NIST has created a methodology—documented in Special Publication (SP) 800-53A, *Guide for Assessing the Security Controls in Federal Information Systems*—which offers suggestions for assessing the effectiveness of the security controls outlined in NIST SP 800-53.[3] Another widely used assessment methodology is the Open Source Security Testing Methodology Manual (OSSTMM).[4] Because there are numerous reasons to conduct assessments, an organization may want to use multiple methodologies. This publication offers recommendations for technical testing and examination techniques that can be used for many assessment methodologies and leveraged for many assessment purposes.

2.2 Technical Assessment Techniques

Dozens of technical security testing and examination techniques exist that can be used to assess the security posture of systems and networks. The most commonly used techniques from the standpoint of this document will be discussed in more depth later in this guide, and are grouped into the following three categories:

- **Review Techniques**. These are examination techniques used to evaluate systems, applications, networks, policies, and procedures to discover vulnerabilities, and are generally conducted manually. They include documentation, log, ruleset, and system configuration review; network sniffing; and file integrity checking. Section 3 provides additional information on review techniques.

- **Target Identification and Analysis Techniques**. These testing techniques can identify systems, ports, services, and potential vulnerabilities, and may be performed manually but are generally performed using automated tools. They include network discovery, network port and service

---

[2] NIST does not endorse one methodology over another; the intent is to provide organizations with options that will allow them to make informed decisions to adopt an existing methodology or combine several to develop a unique methodology that suits the organization.

[3] NIST SP 800-53A discusses the framework for development of assessment procedures, describes the process of assessing security controls, and offers assessment procedures for each control. NIST SP 800-53A was developed to be used in conjunction with NIST SP 800-37, *Guide for the Security Certification and Accreditation of Federal Information Systems*. NIST SPs 800-53, 800-53A, and 800-37 are available at http://csrc.nist.gov/publications/PubsSPs.html.

[4] More information on OSSTMM is available at http://www.isecom.org/osstmm/.

identification, vulnerability scanning, wireless scanning, and application security examination. Further discussion of these techniques is presented in Section 4.

■ **Target Vulnerability Validation Techniques.** These testing techniques corroborate the existence of vulnerabilities, and may be performed manually or by using automatic tools, depending on the specific technique used and the skill of the test team. Target vulnerability validation techniques include password cracking, penetration testing, social engineering, and application security testing. More information on these techniques is found in Section 5.

Since no one technique can provide a complete picture of the security of a system or network, organizations should combine appropriate techniques to ensure robust security assessments. For example, penetration testing usually relies on performing both network port/service identification and vulnerability scanning to identify hosts and services that may be targets for future penetration. Also, multiple technical ways exist to meet an assessment requirement, such as determining whether patches have been applied properly. This publication focuses on explaining *how* these different technical techniques can be performed, and does not specify *which* techniques should be used for which circumstances—thus providing organizations with the flexibility to choose the techniques that best meet their requirements.

In addition to the technical techniques described in this publication, there are many non-technical techniques that may be used in addition to or instead of the technical techniques. One example is physical security testing, which confirms the existence of physical security vulnerabilities by attempting to circumvent locks, badge readers, and other physical security controls, typically to gain unauthorized access to specific hosts. Another example of a non-technical technique is manual asset identification. An organization may choose to identify assets to be assessed through asset inventories, physical walkthroughs of facilities, and other non-technical means, instead of relying on technical techniques for asset identification. Details on non-technical techniques are outside the scope of this publication, but it is important to recognize the value of non-technical techniques and to consider when they may be more appropriate to use than their technical counterparts.

2.3 Comparing Tests and Examinations

Examinations primarily involve the review of documents such as policies, procedures, security plans, security requirements, standard operating procedures, architecture diagrams, engineering documentation, asset inventories, system configurations, rulesets, and system logs. They are conducted to determine whether a system is properly documented, and to gain insight on aspects of security that are only available through documentation. This documentation identifies the intended design, installation, configuration, operation, and maintenance of the systems and network, and its review and cross-referencing ensures conformance and consistency. For example, an environment's security requirements should drive documentation such as system security plans and standard operating procedures—so assessors should ensure that all plans, procedures, architectures, and configurations are compliant with stated security requirements and applicable policies. Another example is reviewing a firewall's ruleset to ensure its compliance with the organization's security policies regarding Internet usage, such as the use of instant messaging, peer-to-peer (P2P) file sharing, and other prohibited activities.

Examinations typically have no impact on the actual systems or networks in the target environment aside from accessing necessary documentation, logs, or rulesets.[5] However, if system configuration files or logs are to be retrieved from a given system such as a router or firewall, only system administrators and

---

[5] One passive testing technique that can potentially impact networks is network sniffing, which involves connecting a sniffer to a hub, tap, or span port on the network. In some cases, the connection process requires reconfiguring a network device, which could disrupt operations.

similarly trained individuals should undertake this work to ensure that settings are not inadvertently modified or deleted.

Testing involves hands-on work with systems and networks to identify security vulnerabilities, and can be executed across an entire enterprise or on selected systems. The use of scanning and penetration techniques can provide valuable information on potential vulnerabilities and predict the likelihood that an adversary or intruder will be able to exploit them. Testing also allows organizations to measure levels of compliance in areas such as patch management, password policy, and configuration management.

Although testing can provide a more accurate picture of an organization's security posture than what is gained through examinations, it is more intrusive and can impact systems or networks in the target environment. The level of potential impact depends on the specific types of testing techniques used, which can interact with the target systems and networks in various ways—such as sending normal network packets to determine open and closed ports, or sending specially crafted packets to test for vulnerabilities. Any time that a test or tester directly interacts with a system or network, the potential exists for unexpected system halts and other denial of service conditions. Organizations should determine their acceptable levels of intrusiveness when deciding which techniques to use. Excluding tests known to create denial of service conditions and other disruptions can help reduce these negative impacts.

Testing does not provide a comprehensive evaluation of the security posture of an organization, and often has a narrow scope because of resource limitations—particularly in the area of time. Malicious attackers, on the other hand, can take whatever time they need to exploit and penetrate a system or network. Also, while organizations tend to avoid using testing techniques that impact systems or networks, attackers are not bound by this constraint and use whatever techniques they feel necessary. As a result, testing is less likely than examinations to identify weaknesses related to security policy and configuration. In many cases, combining testing and examination techniques can provide a more accurate view of security.

2.4 Testing Viewpoints

Tests can be performed from a number of viewpoints—for example, how easily could an external attacker or malicious insider successfully attack a system? Section 2.4.1 of this guide compares testing performed from external and internal viewpoints. Section 2.4.2 discusses another aspect of viewpoints—namely, the previous knowledge that assessors have of the target or target environment.

2.4.1 External and Internal

External security testing is conducted from outside the organization's security perimeter. This offers the ability to view the environment's security posture as it appears outside the security perimeter—usually as seen from the Internet—with the goal of revealing vulnerabilities that could be exploited by an external attacker.

External testing often begins with reconnaissance techniques that search public registration data, Domain Name System (DNS) server information, newsgroup postings, and other publicly available information to collect information (e.g., system names, Internet Protocol [IP] addresses, operating systems, technical points of contact) that may help the assessor to identify vulnerabilities. Next, enumeration begins by using network discovery and scanning techniques to determine external hosts and listening services. Since perimeter defenses such as firewalls, routers, and access control lists often limit the types of traffic allowed into the internal network, assessors often use techniques that evade these defenses—just as external attackers would. Depending on the protocols allowed through, initial attacks are generally focused on commonly used and allowed application protocols such as File Transfer Protocol (FTP), Hypertext Transfer Protocol (HTTP), Simple Mail Transfer Protocol (SMTP), and Post Office Protocol

(POP). Servers that are externally accessible are tested for vulnerabilities that might allow access to internal servers and private information. External security testing also concentrates on discovering access method vulnerabilities, such as wireless access points, modems, and portals to internal servers.

For internal security testing, assessors work from the internal network and assume the identity of a trusted insider or an attacker who has penetrated the perimeter defenses. This kind of testing can reveal vulnerabilities that could be exploited, and demonstrates the potential damage this type of attacker could cause. Internal security testing also focuses on system-level security and configuration—including application and service configuration, authentication, access control, and system hardening.

Assessors who perform internal testing are often granted some level of access to the network, normally as general users, and are provided with information that users with similar privileges would have. This level of temporary access depends on the goals of the test, and can be up to and including the privileges of a system or network administrator. Working from whatever level of access they have been granted, assessors attempt to gain additional access to the network and systems through privilege escalation—i.e., increasing user-level privileges to administrator-level privileges, or increasing system administrator privileges to domain administrator privileges.

Internal testing is not as limited as external testing because it takes place behind perimeter defenses, even though there may be internal firewalls, routers, and switches in place that pose limitations. Examination techniques such as network sniffing may be used in addition to testing techniques.

If both internal and external testing is to be performed, the external testing usually takes place first. This is particularly beneficial if the same assessors will be performing both types of testing, as it keeps them from acquiring insider information on network architecture or system configuration that would not be available to an adversary—an advantage that would reduce the validity of the test.

2.4.2 Overt and Covert

Overt security testing, also known as white hat testing, involves performing external and/or internal testing with the knowledge and consent of the organization's IT staff, enabling comprehensive evaluation of the network or system security posture. Because the IT staff is fully aware of and involved in the testing, it may be able to provide guidance to limit the testing's impact. Testing may also provide a training opportunity, with staff observing the activities and methods used by assessors to evaluate and potentially circumvent implemented security measures. This gives context to the security requirements implemented or maintained by the IT staff, and also may help teach IT staff how to conduct testing.

Covert security testing, also known as black hat testing, takes an adversarial approach by performing testing without the knowledge of the organization's IT staff but with the full knowledge and permission of upper management. Some organizations designate a trusted third party to ensure that the target organization does not initiate response measures associated with the attack without first verifying that an attack is indeed underway (e.g., that the activity being detected does not originate from a test). In such situations, the trusted third party provides an agent for the assessors, the management, the IT staff, and the security staff that mediates activities and facilitates communications. This type of test is useful for testing technical security controls, IT staff response to perceived security incidents, and staff knowledge and implementation of the organization's security policy. Covert testing may be conducted with or without warning.

The purpose of covert testing is to examine the damage or impact an adversary can cause—it does not focus on identifying vulnerabilities. This type of testing does not test every security control, identify each vulnerability, or assess all systems within an organization. Covert testing examines the organization from an adversarial perspective, and normally identifies and exploits the most rudimentary vulnerabilities to gain network access. If an organization's goal is to mirror a specific adversary, this type of testing requires special considerations—such as acquiring and modeling threat data. The resulting scenarios provide an overall strategic view of the potential methods of exploit, risk, and impact of an intrusion. Covert testing usually has defined boundaries, such as stopping testing when a certain level of access is achieved or a certain type of damage is achievable as a next step in testing. Having such boundaries prevents damage while still showing that the damage could occur.

Besides failing to identify many vulnerabilities, covert testing is often time-consuming and costly due to its stealth requirements. To operate in a stealth environment, a test team will have to slow its scans and other actions to stay "under the radar" of the target organization's security staff. When testing is performed in-house, training must also be considered in terms of time and budget. In addition, an organization may have staff trained to perform regular activities such as scanning and vulnerability assessments, but not specialized techniques such as penetration or application security testing. Overt testing is less expensive, carries less risk than covert testing, and is more frequently used—but covert testing provides a better indication of the everyday security of the target organization because system administrators will not have heightened awareness.

3. Review Techniques

Review techniques passively examine systems, applications, networks, policies, and procedures to discover security vulnerabilities.[6] They also gather information to facilitate and optimize other assessment techniques. Because review techniques are passive, they pose minimal risk to systems and networks. This section covers several common review techniques—documentation, log, ruleset, and system configuration review; network sniffing; and file integrity checking.

3.1 Documentation Review

Documentation review determines if the technical aspects of policies and procedures are current and comprehensive. These documents provide the foundation for an organization's security posture, but are often overlooked during technical assessments. Security groups within the organization should provide assessors with appropriate documentation to ensure a comprehensive review. Documents to review for technical accuracy and completeness include security policies, architectures, and requirements; standard operating procedures; system security plans and authorization agreements; memoranda of understanding and agreement for system interconnections; and incident response plans.

Documentation review can discover gaps and weaknesses that could lead to missing or improperly implemented security controls. Assessors typically verify that the organization's documentation is compliant with standards and regulations such as FISMA, and look for policies that are deficient or outdated. Common documentation weaknesses include OS security procedures or protocols that are no longer used, and failure to include a new OS and its protocols. Documentation review does not ensure that security controls are implemented properly—only that the direction and guidance exist to support security infrastructure.

Results of documentation review can be used to fine-tune other testing and examination techniques. For example, if a password management policy has specific requirements for minimum password length and complexity, this information can be used to configure password-cracking tools for more efficient performance.

3.2 Log Review

Log review determines if security controls are logging the proper information, and if the organization is adhering to its log management policies.[7] As a source of historical information, audit logs can be used to help validate that the system is operating in accordance with established policies. For example, if the logging policy states that all authentication attempts to critical servers must be logged, the log review will determine if this information is being collected and shows the appropriate level of detail. Log review may also reveal problems such as misconfigured services and security controls, unauthorized accesses, and attempted intrusions. For example, if an intrusion detection system (IDS) sensor is placed behind a firewall, its logs can be used to examine communications that the firewall allows into the network. If the sensor registers activities that should be blocked, it indicates that the firewall is not configured securely.

---

[6] This publication discusses reviews strictly from the aspect of assessment. Reviews should also be conducted periodically as part of regular system monitoring and maintenance, such as to identify operational problems, security misconfigurations, malicious activity, and other types of security events. Organizations can choose to use findings from operational reviews for their assessments.

[7] NIST SP 800-92, *Guide to Security Log Management*, provides more information on security log management methods and techniques, including log review. It is available at http://csrc.nist.gov/publications/PubsSPs.html.

Examples of log information that may be useful when conducting technical security assessments include:

- Authentication server or system logs may include successful and failed authentication attempts.

- System logs may include system and service startup and shutdown information, installation of unauthorized software, file accesses, security policy changes, account changes (e.g., account creation and deletion, account privilege assignment), and privilege use.

- Intrusion detection and prevention system logs may include malicious activity and inappropriate use.

- Firewall and router logs may include outbound connections that indicate compromised internal devices (e.g., rootkits, bots, Trojan horses, spyware).

- Firewall logs may include unauthorized connection attempts and inappropriate use.

- Application logs may include unauthorized connection attempts, account changes, use of privileges, and application or database usage information.

- Antivirus logs may include update failures and other indications of outdated signatures and software.

- Security logs, in particular patch management and some IDS and intrusion prevention system (IPS) products, may record information on known vulnerable services and applications.

Manually reviewing logs can be extremely time-consuming and cumbersome. Automated audit tools are available that can significantly reduce review time and generate predefined and customized reports that summarize log contents and track them to a set of specific activities. Assessors can also use these automated tools to facilitate log analysis by converting logs in different formats to a single, standard format for analysis. In addition, if assessors are reviewing a specific action—such as the number of failed logon attempts in an organization—they can use these tools to filter logs based on the activity being checked.

3.3   Ruleset Review

A ruleset is a collection of rules or signatures that network traffic or system activity is compared against to determine what action to take—for example, forwarding or rejecting a packet, creating an alert, or allowing a system event. Review of these rulesets is done to ensure comprehensiveness and identify gaps and weaknesses on security devices and throughout layered defenses such as network vulnerabilities, policy violations, and unintended or vulnerable communication paths. A review can also uncover inefficiencies that negatively impact a ruleset's performance.

Rulesets to review include network- and host-based firewall and IDS/IPS rulesets, and router access control lists. The following list provides examples of the types of checks most commonly performed in ruleset reviews:

- For router access control lists

  - Each rule is still required (for example, rules that were added for temporary purposes are removed as soon as they are no longer needed)

  - Only traffic that is authorized per policy is permitted, and all other traffic is denied by default

- For firewall rulesets

- Each rule is still required

- Rules enforce least privilege access, such as specifying only required IP addresses and ports

- More specific rules are triggered before general rules

- There are no unnecessary open ports that could be closed to tighten the perimeter security

- The ruleset does not allow traffic to bypass other security defenses

- For host-based firewall rulesets, the rules do not indicate the presence of backdoors, spyware activity, or prohibited applications such as peer-to-peer file sharing programs

- For IDS/IPS rulesets

  - Unnecessary signatures have been disabled or removed to eliminate false positives and improve performance

  - Necessary signatures are enabled and have been fine-tuned and properly maintained.

3.4 System Configuration Review

System configuration review is the process of identifying weaknesses in security configuration controls, such as systems not being hardened or configured according to security policies. For example, this type of review will reveal unnecessary services and applications, improper user account and password settings, and improper logging and backup settings. Examples of security configuration files that may be reviewed are Windows security policy settings and Unix security configuration files such as those in */etc*.

Assessors using manual review techniques rely on security configuration guides or checklists to verify that system settings are configured to minimize security risks.[8] To perform a manual system configuration review, assessors access various security settings on the device being evaluated and compare them with recommended settings from the checklist. Settings that do not meet minimum security standards are flagged and reported.

The Security Content Automation Protocol (SCAP) is a method for using specific standards to enable automated vulnerability management, measurement, and policy compliance evaluation.[9] NIST SCAP files are written for FISMA compliance and NIST SP 800-53A security control testing. Other tools can be used to retrieve and report security settings and provide remediation guidance. Automated tools are often executed directly on the device being assessed, but can also be executed on a system with network access to the device being assessed. While automated system configuration reviews are faster than manual methods, there may still be settings that must be checked manually. Both manual and automated methods require root or administrator privileges to view selected security settings.

Generally it is preferable to use automated checks instead of manual checks whenever feasible. Automated checks can be done very quickly and provide consistent, repeatable results. Having a person manually checking hundreds or thousands of settings is tedious and error-prone.

---

[8] NIST maintains a repository of security configuration checklists for IT products at http://checklists.nist.gov/.
[9] More information on SCAP is located at http://scap.nist.gov/.

3.5 Network Sniffing

Network sniffing is a passive technique[10] that monitors network communication, decodes protocols, and examines headers and payloads to flag information of interest. Besides being used as a review technique, network sniffing can also be used as a target identification and analysis technique (see Section 4.1). Reasons for using network sniffing include the following:

- Capturing and replaying network traffic

- Performing passive network discovery (e.g., identifying active devices on the network)

- Identifying operating systems, applications, services, and protocols, including unsecured (e.g., telnet) and unauthorized (e.g., peer-to-peer file sharing) protocols

- Identifying unauthorized and inappropriate activities, such as the unencrypted transmission of sensitive information

- Collecting information, such as unencrypted usernames and passwords.

Network sniffing has little impact on systems and networks, with the most noticeable impact being on bandwidth or computing power utilization. The sniffer—the tool used to conduct network sniffing—requires a means to connect to the network, such as a hub, tap, or switch with port spanning. Port spanning is the process of copying the traffic transmitted on all other ports to the port where the sniffer is installed. Organizations can deploy network sniffers in a number of locations within an environment. These commonly include the following:

- At the perimeter, to assess traffic entering and exiting the network

- Behind firewalls, to assess that rulesets are accurately filtering traffic

- Behind IDSs/IPSs, to determine if signatures are triggering and being responded to appropriately

- In front of a critical system or application to assess activity

- On a specific network segment, to validate encrypted protocols.

One limitation to network sniffing is the use of encryption. Many attackers take advantage of encryption to hide their activities—while assessors can see that communication is taking place, they are unable to view the contents. Another limitation is that a network sniffer is only able to sniff the traffic of the local segment where it is installed. This requires the assessor to move it from segment to segment, install multiple sniffers throughout the network, and/or use port spanning. Assessors may also find it challenging to locate an open physical network port for scanning on each segment. In addition, network sniffing is a fairly labor-intensive activity that requires a high degree of human involvement to interpret network traffic.

3.6 File Integrity Checking

File integrity checkers provide a way to identify that system files have been changed computing and storing a checksum for every guarded file, and establishing a file checksum database. Stored checksums are later recomputed to compare their current value with the stored value, which identifies file

---

[10] Sniffers may perform domain name lookups for the traffic they collect, during which they generate network traffic. Domain name lookups can be disabled for stealthy network sniffing.

modifications. A file integrity checker capability is usually included with any commercial host-based IDS, and is also available as a standalone utility.

Although an integrity checker does not require a high degree of human interaction, it must be used carefully to ensure its effectiveness. File integrity checking is most effective when system files are compared with a reference database created using a system known to be secure—this helps ensure that the reference database was not built with compromised files. The reference database should be stored offline to prevent attackers from compromising the system and covering their tracks by modifying the database. In addition, because patches and other updates change files, the checksum database should be kept up-to-date.

For file integrity checking, strong cryptographic checksums such as Secure Hash Algorithm 1 (SHA-1) should be used to ensure the integrity of data stored in the checksum database. Federal agencies are required by Federal Information Processing Standard (FIPS) PUB 140-2, *Security Requirements for Cryptographic Modules*[11], to use SHA (e.g., SHA-1, SHA-256).

3.7 Summary

Table 3-1 summarizes the major capabilities of review techniques discussed in Section 3.

Table 3-1. Review Techniques

Technique	Capabilities
Documentation Review	• Evaluates policies and procedures for technical accuracy and completeness
Log Review	• Provides historical information on system use, configuration, and modification • Could reveal potential problems and policy deviations
Ruleset Review	• Reveals holes in ruleset-based security controls
System Configuration Review	• Evaluates the strength of system configuration • Validates that systems are configured in accordance with hardening policy
Network Sniffing	• Monitors network traffic on the local segment to capture information such as active systems, operating systems, communication protocols, services, and applications • Verifies encryption of communications
File Integrity Checking	• Identifies changes to important files; can also identify certain forms of unwanted files, such as well-known attacker tools

Risks are associated with each technique and their combinations. To ensure that all are executed safely and accurately, each assessor should have a certain baseline skill set. Table 3-2 provides guidelines for the minimum skill set needed for each technique presented in Section 3.

Table 3-2. Baseline Skill Set for Review Techniques

Technique	Baseline Skill Set
Documentation Review	General knowledge of security from a policy perspective
Log Review	Knowledge of log formats and ability to interpret and analyze log data; ability to use automated log analysis and log correlation tools
Ruleset Review	Knowledge of ruleset formats and structures; ability to correlate and analyze rulesets from a variety of devices
System Configuration Review	Knowledge of secure system configuration, including OS hardening and security policy configuration for a variety of operating systems; ability to use automated security configuration testing tools

---

[11] FIPS PUB 140-2 is available at http://csrc.nist.gov/publications/PubsFIPS.html.

Technique	Baseline Skill Set
Network Sniffing	General Transmission Control Protocol/Internet Protocol (TCP/IP) and networking knowledge; ability to interpret and analyze network traffic; ability to deploy and use network sniffing tools
File Integrity Checking	General file system knowledge; ability to use automated file integrity checking tools and interpret the results

4. Target Identification and Analysis Techniques

This section addresses technical target identification and analysis techniques, which focus on identifying active devices and their associated ports and services, and analyzing them for potential vulnerabilities. The assessor uses this information to continue to explore devices that will validate existence of the vulnerabilities. Organizations often use non-technical techniques in addition or instead of technical techniques to identify the assets to be analyzed. For example, organizations may have existing asset inventories or other lists of assets to be targeted; another example is assessors performing a walkthrough of a facility to identify assets that were not found by technical techniques, such as hosts that were shut off or disconnected from the network when the technical techniques were used.

Target identification and analysis techniques for application security examination are briefly discussed in Appendix C.

4.1 Network Discovery

Network discovery uses a number of methods to discover active and responding hosts on a network, identify weaknesses, and learn how the network operates. Both passive (examination) and active (testing) techniques exist for discovering devices on a network. Passive techniques use a network sniffer to monitor network traffic and record the IP addresses of the active hosts, and can report which ports are in use and which operating systems have been discovered on the network. Passive discovery can also identify the relationships between hosts—including which hosts communicate with each other, how frequently their communication occurs, and the type of traffic that is taking place—and is usually performed from a host on the internal network where it can monitor host communications. This is done without sending out a single probing packet. Passive discovery takes more time to gather information than does active discovery, and hosts that do not send or receive traffic during the monitoring period might not be reported.

Active techniques send various types of network packets, such as Internet Control Message Protocol (ICMP) pings, to solicit responses from network hosts, generally through the use of an automated tool. One activity, known as OS fingerprinting, enables the assessor to determine the system's OS by sending it a mix of normal, abnormal, and illegal network traffic. Another activity involves sending packets to common port numbers to generate responses that indicate the ports are active. The tool analyzes the responses from these activities, and compares them with known traits of packets from specific operating systems and network services—enabling it to identify hosts, the operating systems they run, their ports, and the state of those ports. This information can be used for purposes that include gathering information on targets for penetration testing, generating topology maps, determining firewall and IDS configurations, and discovering vulnerabilities in systems and network configurations.

Network discovery tools have many ways to acquire information through scanning. Enterprise firewalls and intrusion detection systems can identify many instances of scans, particularly those that use the most suspicious packets (e.g., SYN/FIN scan, NULL scan). Assessors who plan on performing discovery through firewalls and intrusion detection systems should consider which types of scans are most likely to provide results without drawing the attention of security administrators, and how scans can be conducted in a more stealthy manner (such as more slowly or from a variety of source IP addresses) to improve their chances of success. Assessors should also be cautious when selecting types of scans to use against older systems, particularly those known to have weak security, because some scans can cause system failures. Typically, the closer the scan is to normal activity, the less likely it is to cause operational problems.

Network discovery may also detect unauthorized or rogue devices operating on a network. For example, an organization that uses only a few operating systems could quickly identify rogue devices that utilize different ones. Once a wired rogue device is identified,[12] it can be located by using existing network maps and information already collected on the device's network activity to identify the switch to which it is connected. It may be necessary to generate additional network activity with the rogue device—such as pings—to find the correct switch. The next step is to identify the switch port on the switch associated with the rogue device, and to physically trace the cable connecting that switch port to the rogue device.

A number of tools exist for use in network discovery, and it should be noted that many active discovery tools can be used for passive network sniffing and port scanning as well. Most offer a graphical user interface (GUI), and some also offer a command-line interface. Command-line interfaces may take longer to learn than GUIs because of the number of commands and switches that specify what tests the tool should perform and which an assessor must learn to use the tool effectively. Also, developers have written a number of modules for open source tools that allow assessors to easily parse tool output. For example, combining a tool's Extensible Markup Language (XML) output capabilities, a little scripting, and a database creates a more powerful tool that can monitor the network for unauthorized services and machines. Learning what the many commands do and how to combine them is best achieved with the help of an experienced security engineer. Most experienced IT professionals, including system administrators and other network engineers, should be able to interpret results, but working with the discovery tools themselves is more efficiently handled by an engineer.

Some of the advantages of active discovery, as compared to passive discovery, are that an assessment can be conducted from a different network and usually requires little time to gather information. In passive discovery, ensuring that all hosts are captured requires traffic to hit all points, which can be time-consuming—especially in larger enterprise networks.

A disadvantage to active discovery is that it tends to generate network noise, which sometimes results in network latency. Since active discovery sends out queries to receive responses, this additional network activity could slow down traffic or cause packets to be dropped in poorly configured networks if performed at high volume. Active discovery can also trigger IDS alerts, since unlike passive discovery it reveals its origination point. The ability to successfully discover all network systems can be affected by environments with protected network segments and perimeter security devices and techniques. For example, an environment using network address translation (NAT)—which allows organizations to have internal, non-publicly routed IP addresses that are translated to a different set of public IP addresses for external traffic—may not be accurately discovered from points external to the network or from protected segments. Personal and host-based firewalls on target devices may also block discovery traffic. Misinformation may be received as a result of trying to instigate activity from devices. Active discovery presents information from which conclusions must be drawn about settings on the target network.

For both passive and active discovery, the information received is seldom completely accurate. To illustrate, only hosts that are on and connected during active discovery will be identified—if systems or a segment of the network are offline during the assessment, there is potential for a large gap in discovering devices. Although passive discovery will only find devices that transmit or receive communications during the discovery period, products such as network management software can provide continuous discovery capabilities and automatically generate alerts when a new device is present on the network. Continuous discovery can scan IP address ranges for new addresses or monitor new IP address requests. Also, many discovery tools can be scheduled to run regularly, such as once every set amount of days at a particular time. This provides more accurate results than running these tools sporadically.

---

[12]   See Section 4.4 for information on locating wireless rogue devices.

4.2   Network Port and Service Identification

Network port and service identification involves using a port scanner to identify network ports and services operating on active hosts—such as FTP and HTTP—and the application that is running each identified service, such as Microsoft Internet Information Server (IIS) or Apache for the HTTP service. Organizations should conduct network port and service identification to identify hosts if this has not already been done by other means (e.g., network discovery), and flag potentially vulnerable services. This information can be used to determine targets for penetration testing.

All basic scanners can identify active hosts and open ports, but some scanners are also able to provide additional information on the scanned hosts. Information gathered during an open port scan can assist in identifying the target operating system through a process called *OS fingerprinting*. For example, if a host has TCP ports 135, 139, and 445 open, it is probably a Windows host, or possibly a Unix host running Samba. Other items—such as the TCP packet sequence number generation and responses to packets—also provide a clue to identifying the OS. But OS fingerprinting is not foolproof. For example, firewalls block certain ports and types of traffic, and system administrators can configure their systems to respond in nonstandard ways to camouflage the true OS.

Some scanners can help identify the application running on a particular port through a process called service identification. Many scanners use a services file that lists common port numbers and typical associated services—for example, a scanner that identifies that TCP port 80 is open on a host may report that a web server is listening at that port—but additional steps are needed before this can be confirmed. Some scanners can initiate communications with an observed port and analyze its communications to determine what service is there, often by comparing the observed activity to a repository of information on common services and service implementations. These techniques may also be used to identify the service application and application version, such as which Web server software is in use—this process is known as *version scanning*. A well-known form of version scanning, called *banner grabbing*, involves capturing banner information transmitted by the remote port when a connection is initiated. This information can include the application type, application version, and even OS type and version. Version scanning is not foolproof, because a security-conscious administrator can alter the transmitted banners or other characteristics in hopes of concealing the service's true nature. However, version scanning is far more accurate than simply relying on a scanner's services file.

Scanner models support the various scanning methods with strengths and weaknesses that are normally explained in their documentation. For example, some scanners work best scanning through firewalls, while others are better suited for scans inside the firewall. Results will differ depending on the port scanner used. Some scanners respond with a simple open or closed response for each port, while others offer additional detail (e.g., filtered or unfiltered) that can assist the assessor in determining what other types of scans would be helpful to gain additional information.

Network port and service identification often uses the IP address results of network discovery as the devices to scan. Port scans can also be run independently on entire blocks of IP addresses—here, port scanning performs network discovery by default through identifying the active hosts on the network. The result of network discovery and network port and service identification is a list of all active devices operating in the address space that responded to the port scanning tool, along with responding ports. Additional active devices could exist that did not respond to scanning, such as those that are shielded by firewalls or turned off. Assessors can try to find these devices by scanning the devices themselves, placing the scanner on a segment that can access the devices, or attempting to evade the firewall through the use of alternate scan types (e.g., SYN/FIN or Xmas scan).[13]

It is recommended that if both external and internal scanning are to be used and the assessors are intentionally performing the testing "blind," that external scanning be performed first. Done in this order, logs can be reviewed and compared before and during internal testing. When performing external scanning, assessors may use any existing stealth techniques to get packets through firewalls while evading detection by IDS and IPS.[14] Tools that use fragmentation, duplication, overlap, out-of-order, and timing techniques to alter packets so that they blend into and appear more like normal traffic are recommended. Internal testing tends to use less aggressive scanning methods because these scans are blocked less often than external scans. Using more aggressive scans internally significantly increases the changes of disrupting operations without necessarily improving scan results. Being able to scan a network with customized packets also works well for internal testing, because checking for specific vulnerabilities requires highly customized packets. Tools with packet-builder ability are helpful with this process. Once built, packets can be sent through a second scanning program that will collect the results. Because customized packets can trigger a denial of service (DoS) attack, this type of test should be conducted during periods of low network traffic—such as overnight or on the weekend.

Although port scanners identify active hosts, operating systems, ports, services, and applications, they do not identify vulnerabilities. Additional investigation is needed to confirm the presence of insecure protocols (e.g., Trivial File Transfer Protocol [TFTP], telnet), malware, unauthorized applications, and vulnerable services. To identify vulnerable services, the assessor compares identified version numbers of services with a list of known vulnerable versions, or perform automated vulnerability scanning as discussed in Section 4.3. With port scanners, the scanning process is highly automated but interpretation of the scanned data is not.

Although port scanning can disrupt network operations by consuming bandwidth and slowing network response times, it enables an organization to ensure that its hosts are configured to run only approved network services. Scanning software should be carefully selected to minimize disruptions to operations. Port scanning can also be conducted after hours to cause minimal impact to operations.

4.3 Vulnerability Scanning

Like network port and service identification, vulnerability scanning identifies hosts and host attributes (e.g., operating systems, applications, open ports), but it also attempts to identify vulnerabilities rather than relying on human interpretation of the scanning results. Many vulnerability scanners are equipped to accept results from network discovery and network port and service identification, which reduces the amount of work needed for vulnerability scanning. Also, some scanners can perform their own network discovery and network port and service identification. Vulnerability scanning can help identify outdated software versions, missing patches, and misconfigurations, and validate compliance with or deviations from an organization's security policy. This is done by identifying the operating systems and major software applications running on the hosts and matching them with information on known vulnerabilities stored in the scanners' vulnerability databases.

Vulnerability scanners can:

■ Check compliance with host application usage and security policies

---

[13] Many firewalls can recognize and block various alternate scan types, so testers may not be able to use them to evade firewalls in many environments.

[14] This can be particularly helpful in improving the tuning and configuration of IDSs and IPSs.

■ Provide information on targets for penetration testing

■ Provide information on how to mitigate discovered vulnerabilities.

Vulnerability scanners can be run against a host either locally or from the network. Some network-based scanners have administrator-level credentials on individual hosts and can extract vulnerability information from hosts using those credentials. Other network-based scanners do not have such credentials and must rely on conducting scanning of networks to locate hosts and then scan those hosts for vulnerabilities. In such cases, network-based scanning is primarily used to perform network discovery and identify open ports and related vulnerabilities—in most cases, it is not limited by the OS of the targeted systems. Network-based scanning without host credentials can be performed both internally and externally—and although internal scanning usually uncovers more vulnerabilities than external scanning, testing from both viewpoints is important. External scanning must contend with perimeter security devices that block traffic, limiting assessors to scanning only the ports authorized to pass traffic.

Assessors performing external scanning may find challenges similar to those faced with network discovery, such as the use of NAT or personal and host-based firewalls. To overcome the challenges of NAT and conduct successful network-based scanning, assessors can ask the firewall administrator to enable port forwarding on specific IP addresses or groups of addresses if this is supported by the firewall, or request network access behind the device performing NAT. Assessors can also request that personal or host-based firewalls be configured to permit traffic from test system IP addresses during the assessment period. These steps will give assessors increased insight into the network, but do not accurately reflect the capabilities of an external attacker—although they may offer a better indication of the capabilities available to a malicious insider or an external attacker with access to another host on the internal network. Assessors can also perform scanning on individual hosts.

For local vulnerability scanning, a scanner is installed on each host to be scanned. This is done primarily to identify host OS and application misconfigurations and vulnerabilities—both network-exploitable and locally exploitable. Local scanning is able to detect vulnerabilities with a higher level of detail than network-based scanning because local scanning usually requires both host (local) access and a root or administrative account. Some scanners also offer the capability of repairing local misconfigurations.

A vulnerability scanner is a relatively fast and easy way to quantify an organization's exposure to surface vulnerabilities. A surface vulnerability is a weakness that exists in isolation, independent from other vulnerabilities. The system's behaviors and outputs in response to attack patterns submitted by the scanner are compared against those that characterize the signatures of known vulnerabilities, and the tool reports any matches that are found. Besides signature-based scanning, some vulnerability scanners attempt to simulate the reconnaissance attack patterns used to probe for exposed, exploitable vulnerabilities, and report the vulnerabilities found when these techniques are successful.

One difficulty in identifying the risk level of vulnerabilities is that they rarely exist in isolation. For example, there could be several low-risk vulnerabilities that present a higher risk when combined. Scanners are unable to detect vulnerabilities that are revealed only as the result of potentially unending combinations of attack patterns. The tool may assign a low risk to each vulnerability, leaving the assessor falsely confident in the security measures in place. A more reliable way of identifying the risk of vulnerabilities in aggregate is through penetration testing, which is discussed in Section 5.2.

Another problem with identifying the risk level of vulnerabilities is that vulnerability scanners often use their own proprietary methods for defining the levels. For example, one scanner might use the levels low, medium, and high, while another scanner might use the levels informational, low, medium, high, and critical. This makes it difficult to compare findings among multiple scanners. Also, the risk levels assigned by a scanner may not reflect the actual risk to the organization—for example, a scanner might label an FTP server as a moderate risk because it transmits passwords in cleartext, but if the organization only uses the FTP server as an anonymous public server that does not use passwords, then the actual risk might be considerably lower. Assessors should determine the appropriate risk level for each vulnerability and not simply accept the risk levels assigned by vulnerability scanners.

Network-based vulnerability scanning has some significant weaknesses. As with network sniffing and discovery, this type of scanning uncovers vulnerabilities only for active systems. This generally covers surface vulnerabilities, and is unable to address the overall risk level of a scanned network. Although the process itself is highly automated, vulnerability scanners can have a high false positive error rate (i.e., reporting vulnerabilities when none exist). An individual with expertise in networking and OS security should interpret the results. And because network-based vulnerability scanning requires more information than port scanning to reliably identify the vulnerabilities on a host, it tends to generate significantly more network traffic than port scanning. This may have a negative impact on the hosts or network being scanned, or on network segments through which scanning traffic is traversing. Many vulnerability scanners also include network-based tests for DoS attacks that, in the hands of an inexperienced assessor, can have a marked negative impact on scanned hosts. Scanners often allow all DoS attack tests to be suppressed so as to reduce the risk of impacting hosts through testing.

Another significant limitation of vulnerability scanners is that, like virus scanners and IDSs, they rely on a repository of signatures. This requires the assessors to update these signatures frequently to enable the scanner to recognize the latest vulnerabilities. Before running any scanner, an assessor should install the latest updates to its vulnerability database. Some vulnerability scanner databases are updated more regularly than others—this update frequency should be a major consideration when selecting a vulnerability scanner.

Most vulnerability scanners allow the assessor to perform different levels of scanning that vary in terms of thoroughness. While more comprehensive scanning may detect a greater number of vulnerabilities, it can slow the overall scanning process. Less comprehensive scanning can take less time, but identifies only well-known vulnerabilities. It is generally recommended that assessors conduct a thorough vulnerability scan if resources permit.

Vulnerability scanning is a somewhat labor-intensive activity that requires a high degree of human involvement to interpret results. It may also disrupt network operations by taking up bandwidth and slowing response times. Nevertheless, vulnerability scanning is extremely important in ensuring that vulnerabilities are mitigated before they are discovered and exploited by adversaries.

As with all pattern-matching and signature-based tools, application vulnerability scanners typically have high false positive rates. Assessors should configure and calibrate their scanners to minimize both false positives and false negatives to the greatest possible extent, and meaningfully interpret results to identify the real vulnerabilities. Scanners also suffer from the high false negative rates that characterize other signature-based tools—but vulnerabilities that go undetected by automated scanners can potentially be caught using multiple vulnerability scanners or additional forms of testing. A common practice is to use multiple scanners—this provides assessors with a way to compare results.

4.4 Wireless Scanning

Wireless technologies, in their simplest sense, enable one or more devices to communicate without the need for physical connections such as network or peripheral cables. They range from simple technologies like wireless keyboards and mice to complex cell phone networks and enterprise wireless local area networks (WLAN). As the number and availability of wireless-enabled devices continues to increase, it

is important for organizations to actively test and secure their enterprise wireless environments.[15]
Wireless scans can help organizations determine corrective actions to mitigate risks posed by wireless-enabled technologies.

The following factors in the organization's environment should be taken into consideration when planning technical wireless security assessments:

■ The location of the facility being scanned, because the physical proximity of a building to a public area (e.g., streets and public common areas) or its location in a busy metropolitan area may increase the risk of wireless threats

■ The security level of the data to be transmitted using wireless technologies

■ How often wireless devices connect to and disconnect from the environment, and the typical traffic levels for wireless devices (e.g., occasional activity or fairly constant activity)—this is because only active wireless devices are discoverable during a wireless scan

■ Existing deployments of wireless intrusion detection and prevention systems (WIDPS[16]), which may already collect most of the information that would be gathered by testing.

Wireless scanning should be conducted using a mobile device with wireless analyzer software installed and configured—such as a laptop, handheld device, or specialty device. The scanning software or tool should allow the operator to configure the device for specific scans, and to scan in both passive and active modes. The scanning software should also be configurable by the operator to identify deviations from the organization's wireless security configuration requirements.

The wireless scanning tool should be capable of scanning all Institute of Electrical and Electronics Engineers (IEEE) 802.11a/b/g/n channels, whether domestic or international. In some cases, the device should also be fitted with an external antenna to provide an additional level of radio frequency (RF) capturing capability. Support for other wireless technologies, such as Bluetooth, will help evaluate the presence of additional wireless threats and vulnerabilities. Note that devices using nonstandard technology or frequencies outside of the scanning tool's RF range will not be detected or properly recognized by the scanning tool. A tool such as an RF spectrum analyzer will assist organizations in identifying transmissions that occur within the frequency range of the spectrum analyzer. Spectrum analyzers generally analyze a large frequency range (e.g., 3 to 18 GHz) —and although these devices do not analyze traffic, they enable an assessor to determine wireless activity within a specific frequency range and tailor additional testing and examination accordingly.

Some devices also support mapping and physical location plotting through use of a mapping tool, and in some cases support Global Positioning System (GPS)-based mapping. Sophisticated wireless scanning tools allow the user to import a floor plan or map to assist in plotting the physical location of discovered devices. (It is important to note that GPS has limited capabilities indoors.)

Individuals with a strong understanding of wireless networking—especially IEEE 802.11a/b/g/n technologies—should operate wireless scanning tools. These operators should be trained on the functionality and capability of the scanning tools and software to better understand the captured information and be more apt to identify potential threats or malicious activity. Individuals with similar

---

[15] For proper measures to secure IEEE 802.11-based WLANs, please refer to NIST SP 800-97, *Establishing Wireless Robust Security Networks: A Guide to IEEE 802.11i,* and NIST SP 800-48 Revision 1, *Guide to Securing Legacy IEEE 802.11 Wireless Networks,* available at http://csrc.nist.gov/publications/PubsSPs.html.

[16] For more information, see NIST SP 800-94, *Guide to Intrusion Detection and Prevention Systems (IDPS),* which is available at http://csrc.nist.gov/publications/PubsSPs.html.

skills should be employed to analyze the data and results acquired from wireless scans. Scanning tool operators should be aware of other RF signals authorized for use within the area being scanned.

4.4.1 Passive Wireless Scanning

Passive scanning should be conducted regularly to supplement wireless security measures already in place, such as WIDPSs.[17] Wireless scanning tools used to conduct completely passive scans transmit no data, nor do the tools in any way affect the operation of deployed wireless devices. By not transmitting data, a passive scanning tool remains undetected by malicious users and other devices. This reduces the likelihood of individuals avoiding detection by disconnecting or disabling unauthorized wireless devices.

Passive scanning tools capture wireless traffic being transmitted within the range of the tool's antenna. Most tools provide several key attributes regarding discovered wireless devices, including service set identifier (SSID), device type, channel, media access control (MAC) address, signal strength, and number of packets being transmitted. This information can be used to evaluate the security of the wireless environment, and to identify potential rogue devices and unauthorized ad hoc networks discovered within range of the scanning device. The wireless scanning tool should also be able to assess the captured packets to determine if any operational anomalies or threats exist.

Wireless scanning tools scan each IEEE 802.11a/b/g/n channel/frequency separately, often for only several hundred milliseconds at a time. The passive scanning tool may not receive all transmissions on a specific channel. For example, the tool may have been scanning channel 1 at the precise moment when a wireless device transmitted a packet on channel 5. This makes it important to set the dwell time of the tool to be long enough to capture packets, yet short enough to efficiently scan each channel. Dwell time configurations will depend on the device or tool used to conduct the wireless scans. In addition, security personnel conducting the scans should slowly move through the area being scanned to reduce the number of devices that go undetected.

Rogue devices can be identified in several ways through passive scanning:

- The MAC address of a discovered wireless device indicates the vendor of the device's wireless interface. If an organization only deploys wireless interfaces from vendors A and B, the presence of interfaces from any other vendor indicates potential rogue devices.

- If an organization has accurate records of its deployed wireless devices, assessors can compare the MAC addresses of discovered devices with the MAC addresses of authorized devices. Most scanning tools allow assessors to enter a list of authorized devices. Because MAC addresses can be spoofed, assessors should not assume that the MAC addresses of discovered devices are accurate—but checking MAC addresses can identify rogue devices that do not use spoofing.

- Rogue devices may use SSIDs that are not authorized by the organization.

- Some rogue devices may use SSIDs that are authorized by the organization but do not adhere to its wireless security configuration requirements.

The signal strength of potential rogue devices should be reviewed to determine whether the devices are located within the confines of the facility or in the area being scanned. Devices operating outside an

---

[17] In some environments, the WIDPS implementation might be performing most of the same functions as passive wireless scanning. Some WIDPS products offer mobile sensors similar to the wireless scanning device setup described in Section 4.4. Organizations with WIDPS implementations should use the wireless scanning techniques described in this publication to supplement, not duplicate, WIDPS functionality.

organization's confines might still pose significant risks because the organization's devices might inadvertently associate to them.

4.4.2   Active Wireless Scanning

Organizations can move beyond passive wireless scanning to conduct active scanning. This builds on the information collected during passive scans, and attempts to attach to discovered devices and conduct penetration or vulnerability-related testing. For example, organizations can conduct active wireless scanning on their authorized wireless devices to ensure that they meet wireless security configuration requirements—including authentication mechanisms, data encryption, and administration access if this information is not already available through other means.

Organizations should be cautious in conducting active scans to make sure they do not inadvertently scan devices owned or operated by neighboring organizations that are within range. It is important to evaluate the physical location of devices before actively scanning them. Organizations should also be cautious in performing active scans of rogue devices that appear to be operating within the organization's facility. Such devices could belong to a visitor to the organization who inadvertently has wireless access enabled, or to a neighboring organization with a device that is close to, but not within, the organization's facility. Generally, organizations should focus on identifying and locating potential rogue devices rather than performing active scans of such devices.

Organizations may use active scanning when conducting penetration testing on their own wireless devices. Tools are available that employ scripted attacks and functions, attempt to circumvent implemented security measures, and evaluate the security level of devices. For example, tools used to conduct wireless penetration testing attempt to connect to access points (AP) through various methods to circumvent security configurations. If the tool can gain access to the AP, it can obtain information and identify the wired networks and wireless devices to which the AP is connected. Some active tools may also identify vulnerabilities discovered on the wireless client devices, or conduct wired network vulnerability tests as outlined in Section 4.

While active scanning is being performed, the organization's WIDPSs can be monitored to evaluate their capabilities and performance. Depending on assessment goals, assessors conducting these scans may need to inform the WIDPS administrators and wireless network administrators of pending scanning to prepare them for possible alarms and alerts. In addition, some WIDPSs can be configured to ignore alarms and alerts triggered by a specific device—such as one used to perform scanning.

Tools and processes to identify unauthorized devices and vulnerabilities on wired networks can also be used to identify rogue and misconfigured wireless devices. Wired-side scanning is another process that can be conducted to discover, and possibly locate, rogue wireless devices. Sections 3.5 and 4.1 discuss wired scanning.

4.4.3   Wireless Device Location Tracking

Security personnel who operate the wireless scanning tool should attempt to locate suspicious devices. RF signals propagate in a manner relative to the environment, which makes it important for the operator to understand how wireless technology supports this process. Mapping capabilities are useful here, but the main factors needed to support this capability are a knowledgeable operator and an appropriate wireless antenna.

If rogue devices are discovered and physically located during the wireless scan, security personnel should ensure that specific policies and processes are followed on how the rogue device is handled—such as shutting it down, reconfiguring it to comply with the organization's policies, or removing the device completely. If the device is to be removed, security personnel should evaluate the activity of the rogue device before it is confiscated. This can be done through monitoring transmissions and attempting to access the device.

If discovered wireless devices cannot be located during the scan, security personnel should attempt to use a WIDPS to support the location of discovered devices. This requires the WIDPS to locate a specific MAC address that was discovered during the scan. Properly deployed WIDPSs should have the ability to assist security personnel in locating these devices, and usually involves the use of multiple WIDPS sensors to increase location identification granularity. Because the WIDPS will only be able to locate a device within several feet, a wireless scanning tool may still be needed to pinpoint the location of the device.

4.4.4 Bluetooth Scanning

For organizations that want to confirm compliance with their Bluetooth security requirements, passive scanning for Bluetooth-enabled wireless devices should be conducted to evaluate potential presence and activity. Because Bluetooth has a very short range (on average 9 meters [30 feet], with some devices having ranges of as little as 1 meter [3 feet]), scanning for devices can be difficult and time-consuming. Assessors should take range limitations into consideration when scoping this type of scanning. Organizations may want to perform scanning only in areas of their facilities that are accessible by the public—to see if attackers could gain access to devices via Bluetooth—or to perform scanning in a sampling of physical locations rather than throughout the entire facility. Because many Bluetooth-enabled devices (such as cell phones and personal digital assistants [PDA]) are mobile, conducting passive scanning several times over a period of time may be necessary. Organizations should also scan any Bluetooth infrastructure, such as access points, that they deploy. If rogue access points are discovered, the organization should handle them in accordance with established policies and processes.

A number of tools are available for actively testing the security and operation of Bluetooth devices. These tools attempt to connect to discovered devices and perform attacks to surreptitiously gain access and connectivity to Bluetooth-enabled devices. Assessors should be extremely cautious of performing active scanning because of the likelihood of inadvertently scanning personal Bluetooth devices, which are found in many environments. As a general rule, assessors should use active scanning only when they are certain that the devices being scanned belong to the organization. Active scanning can be used to evaluate the security mode in which a Bluetooth device is operating, and the strength of Bluetooth password identification numbers (PIN). Active scanning can also be used to verify that these devices are set to the lowest possible operational power setting to minimize their range. As with IEEE 802.11a/b/g rogue devices, rogue Bluetooth devices should be dealt with in accordance with policies and guidance.

4.5 Summary

Table 4-1 summarizes the major capabilities of the target identification and analysis techniques discussed in Section 4.

Table 4-1. Target Identification and Analysis Techniques

Technique	Capabilities
Network Discovery	• Discovers active devices • Identifies communication paths and facilitates determination of network architectures
Network Port and Service Identification	• Discovers active devices • Discovers open ports and associated services/ applications

Technique	Capabilities
Vulnerability Scanning	• Identifies hosts and open ports • Identifies known vulnerabilities (note: has high false positive rates) • Often provides advice on mitigating discovered vulnerabilities
Wireless Scanning	• Identifies unauthorized wireless devices within range of the scanners • Discovers wireless signals outside of an organization's perimeter • Detects potential backdoors and other security violations

There are risks associated with each technique and combination of techniques. To ensure that all are executed safely and accurately, each assessor should have a certain baseline skill set. Table 4-2 provides guidelines for the minimum skill set needed for each technique presented in Section 4.

Table 4-2. Baseline Skill Set for Target Identification and Analysis Techniques

Technique	Baseline Skill Set
Network Discovery	General TCP/IP and networking knowledge; ability to use both passive and active network discovery tools
Network Port and Service Identification	General TCP/IP and networking knowledge; knowledge of ports and protocols for a variety of operating systems; ability to use port scanning tools; ability to interpret results from tools
Vulnerability Scanning	General TCP/IP and networking knowledge; knowledge of ports, protocols, services, and vulnerabilities for a variety of operating systems; ability to use automated vulnerability scanning tools and interpret/analyze the results
Wireless Scanning	General knowledge of computing and radio transmissions in addition to specific knowledge of wireless protocols, services, and architectures; ability to use automated wireless scanning and sniffing tools

5.   Target Vulnerability Validation Techniques

This section addresses target vulnerability validation techniques, which use information produced from target identification and analysis to further explore the existence of potential vulnerabilities. The objective is to prove that a vulnerability exists, and to demonstrate the security exposures that occur when it is exploited. Target vulnerability validation involves the greatest amount of risk in assessments, since these techniques have more potential to impact the target system or network than other techniques.

Target vulnerability validation techniques for application security testing are briefly discussed in Appendix C.

5.1   Password Cracking

When a user enters a password, a hash of the entered password is generated and compared with a stored hash of the user's actual password. If the hashes match, the user is authenticated. Password cracking is the process of recovering passwords from password hashes stored in a computer system or transmitted over networks. It is usually performed during assessments to identify accounts with weak passwords. Password cracking is performed on hashes that are either intercepted by a network sniffer while being transmitted across a network, or retrieved from the target system, which generally requires administrative-level access on, or physical access to, the target system. Once these hashes are obtained, an automated password cracker rapidly generates additional hashes until a match is found or the assessor halts the cracking attempt.

One method for generating hashes is a *dictionary attack*, which uses all words in a dictionary or text file. There are numerous dictionaries available on the Internet that encompass major and minor languages, names, popular television shows, etc. Another cracking method is known as a *hybrid attack*, which builds on the dictionary method by adding numeric and symbolic characters to dictionary words. Depending on the password cracker being used, this type of attack can try a number of variations, such as using common substitutions of characters and numbers for letters (e.g., p@ssword and h4ckme). Some will also try adding characters and numbers to the beginning and end of dictionary words (e.g., password99, password$%).

Yet another password-cracking method is called the *brute force* method. This generates all possible passwords up to a certain length and their associated hashes. Since there are so many possibilities, it can take months to crack a password. Although brute force can take a long time, it usually takes far less time than most password policies specify for password changing. Consequently, passwords found during brute force attacks are still too weak. Theoretically, all passwords can be cracked by a brute force attack, given enough time and processing power, although it could take many years and require serious computing power. Assessors and attackers often have multiple machines over which they can spread the task of cracking passwords, which greatly shortens the time involved.

Password cracking can also be performed with *rainbow tables*, which are lookup tables with pre-computed password hashes. For example, a rainbow table can be created that contains every possible password for a given character set up to a certain character length. Assessors may then search the table for the password hashes that they are trying to crack. Rainbow tables require large amounts of storage space and can take a long time to generate, but their primary shortcoming is that they may be ineffective against password hashing that uses *salting*. Salting is the inclusion of a random piece of information in the password hashing process that decreases the likelihood of identical passwords returning the same hash. Rainbow tables will not produce correct results without taking salting into account—but this dramatically increases the amount of storage space that the tables require. Many operating systems use salted password hashing mechanisms to reduce the effectiveness of rainbow tables and other forms of password cracking.

Password crackers can be run during an assessment to ensure policy compliance by verifying acceptable password composition. For example, if the organization has a password expiration policy, then password crackers can be run at intervals that coincide with the intended password lifetime. Password cracking that is performed offline produces little or no impact on the system or network, and the benefits of this operation include validating the organization's password policy and verifying policy compliance.

5.2 Penetration Testing

Penetration testing is security testing in which assessors mimic real-world attacks to identify methods for circumventing the security features of an application, system, or network. It often involves launching real attacks on real systems and data that use tools and techniques commonly used by attackers. Most penetration tests involve looking for combinations of vulnerabilities on one or more systems that can be used to gain more access than could be achieved through a single vulnerability. Penetration testing can also be useful for determining:

- How well the system tolerates real world-style attack patterns

- The likely level of sophistication an attacker needs to successfully compromise the system

- Additional countermeasures that could mitigate threats against the system

- Defenders' ability to detect attacks and respond appropriately.

Penetration testing can be invaluable, but it is labor-intensive and requires great expertise to minimize the risk to targeted systems. Systems may be damaged or otherwise rendered inoperable during the course of penetration testing, even though the organization benefits in knowing how a system could be rendered inoperable by an intruder. Although experienced penetration testers can mitigate this risk, it can never be fully eliminated. Penetration testing should be performed only after careful consideration, notification, and planning.

Penetration testing often includes non-technical methods of attack. For example, a penetration tester could breach physical security controls and procedures to connect to a network, steal equipment, capture sensitive information (possibly by installing keylogging devices), or disrupt communications. Caution should be exercised when performing physical security testing—security guards should be made aware of how to verify the validity of tester activity, such as via a point of contact or documentation. Another non-technical means of attack is the use of social engineering, such as posing as a help desk agent and calling to request a user's passwords, or calling the help desk posing as a user and asking for a password to be reset. Additional information on physical security testing, social engineering techniques, and other non-technical means of attack included in penetration testing lies outside the scope of this publication.

5.2.1 Penetration Testing Phases

Figure 5-1 represents the four phases of penetration testing.[18] In the planning phase, rules are identified, management approval is finalized and documented, and testing goals are set. The planning phase sets the groundwork for a successful penetration test. No actual testing occurs in this phase.

---

[18] This is an example of how the penetration process can be divided into phases. There are many acceptable ways of grouping the actions involved in performing penetration testing.

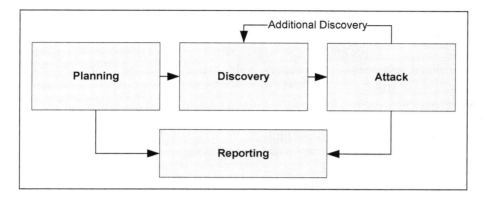

Figure 5-1. Four-Stage Penetration Testing Methodology

The discovery phase of penetration testing includes two parts. The first part is the start of actual testing, and covers information gathering and scanning. Network port and service identification, described in Section 4.2, is conducted to identify potential targets. In addition to port and service identification, other techniques are used to gather information on the targeted network:

- **Host name and IP address information** can be gathered through many methods, including DNS interrogation, InterNIC (WHOIS) queries, and network sniffing (generally only during internal tests)

- **Employee names and contact information** can be obtained by searching the organization's Web servers or directory servers

- **System information, such as names and shares** can be found through methods such as NetBIOS enumeration (generally only during internal tests) and Network Information System (NIS) (generally only during internal tests)

- **Application and service information,** such as version numbers, can be recorded through banner grabbing.

In some cases, techniques such as dumpster diving and physical walkthroughs of facilities may be used to collect additional information on the targeted network, and may also uncover additional information to be used during the penetration tests, such as passwords written on paper.

The second part of the discovery phase is vulnerability analysis, which involves comparing the services, applications, and operating systems of scanned hosts against vulnerability databases (a process that is automatic for vulnerability scanners) and the testers' own knowledge of vulnerabilities. Human testers can use their own databases—or public databases such as the National Vulnerability Database (NVD) — to identify vulnerabilities manually. Appendix E has more information on these publicly available vulnerability databases. Manual processes can identify new or obscure vulnerabilities that automated scanners may miss, but are much slower than an automated scanner.

Executing an attack is at the heart of any penetration test. Figure 5-2 represents the individual steps of the attack phase—the process of verifying previously identified potential vulnerabilities by attempting to exploit them. If an attack is successful, the vulnerability is verified and safeguards are identified to mitigate the associated security exposure. In many cases, exploits[19] that are executed do not grant the

---

[19]   Exploit programs or scripts are specialized tools for exploiting specific vulnerabilities. The same cautions that apply to freeware tools apply to exploit programs and scripts. Some vulnerability databases, including Bugtraq (available at http://www.securityfocus.com/) provide exploit instructions or code for many identified vulnerabilities.

maximum level of potential access to an attacker. They may instead result in the testers learning more about the targeted network and its potential vulnerabilities, or induce a change in the state of the targeted network's security. Some exploits enable testers to escalate their privileges on the system or network to gain access to additional resources. If this occurs, additional analysis and testing are required to determine the true level of risk for the network, such as identifying the types of information that can be gleaned, changed, or removed from the system. In the event an attack on a specific vulnerability proves impossible, the tester should attempt to exploit another discovered vulnerability. If testers are able to exploit a vulnerability, they can install more tools on the target system or network to facilitate the testing process. These tools are used to gain access to additional systems or resources on the network, and obtain access to information about the network or organization. Testing and analysis on multiple systems should be conducted during a penetration test to determine the level of access an adversary could gain. This process is represented in the feedback loop in Figure 5-1 between the attack and discovery phase of a penetration test.

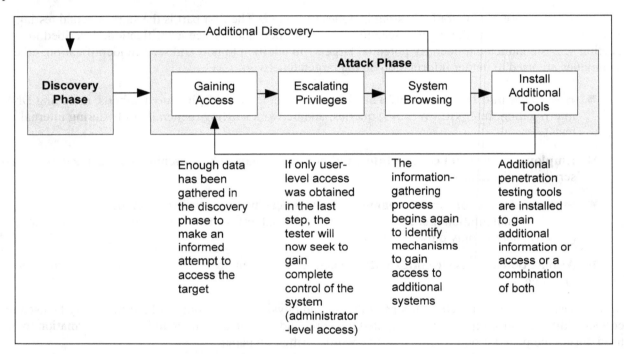

Figure 5-2. Attack Phase Steps with Loopback to Discovery Phase

While vulnerability scanners check only for the possible existence of a vulnerability, the attack phase of a penetration test exploits the vulnerability to confirm its existence. Most vulnerabilities exploited by penetration testing fall into the following categories:

- **Misconfigurations.** Misconfigured security settings, particularly insecure default settings, are usually easily exploitable.

- **Kernel Flaws.** Kernel code is the core of an OS, and enforces the overall security model for the system—so any security flaw in the kernel puts the entire system in danger.

- **Buffer Overflows.** A buffer overflow occurs when programs do not adequately check input for appropriate length. When this occurs, arbitrary code can be introduced into the system and executed with the privileges—often at the administrative level—of the running program.

- **Insufficient Input Validation.** Many applications fail to fully validate the input they receive from users. An example is a Web application that embeds a value from a user in a database query. If the user enters SQL commands instead of or in addition to the requested value, and the Web application does not filter the SQL commands, the query may be run with malicious changes that the user requested—causing what is known as a SQL injection attack.

- **Symbolic Links.** A symbolic link (symlink) is a file that points to another file. Operating systems include programs that can change the permissions granted to a file. If these programs run with privileged permissions, a user could strategically create symlinks to trick these programs into modifying or listing critical system files.

- **File Descriptor Attacks.** File descriptors are numbers used by the system to keep track of files in lieu of filenames. Specific types of file descriptors have implied uses. When a privileged program assigns an inappropriate file descriptor, it exposes that file to compromise.

- **Race Conditions.** Race conditions can occur during the time a program or process has entered into a privileged mode. A user can time an attack to take advantage of elevated privileges while the program or process is still in the privileged mode.

- **Incorrect File and Directory Permissions.** File and directory permissions control the access assigned to users and processes. Poor permissions could allow many types of attacks, including the reading or writing of password files or additions to the list of trusted remote hosts.

The reporting phase occurs simultaneously with the other three phases of the penetration test (see Figure 5-1). In the planning phase, the assessment plan—or ROE—is developed. In the discovery and attack phases, written logs are usually kept and periodic reports are made to system administrators and/or management. At the conclusion of the test, a report is generally developed to describe identified vulnerabilities, present a risk rating, and give guidance on how to mitigate the discovered weaknesses. Section 8 discusses post-testing activities such as reporting in more detail.

5.2.2 Penetration Testing Logistics

Penetration test scenarios should focus on locating and targeting exploitable defects in the design and implementation of an application, system, or network. Tests should reproduce both the most likely and most damaging attack patterns—including worst-case scenarios such as malicious actions by administrators. Since a penetration test scenario can be designed to simulate an inside attack, an outside attack, or both, external and internal security testing methods are considered. If both internal and external testing is to be performed, the external testing usually occurs first.

Outsider scenarios simulate the outsider-attacker who has little or no specific knowledge of the target and who works entirely from assumptions. To simulate an external attack, testers are provided with no real information about the target environment other than targeted IP addresses or address ranges,[20] and perform open source research by collecting information on the targets from public Web pages, newsgroups, and similar sites. Port scanners and vulnerability scanners are then used to identify target hosts. Since the testers' traffic usually goes through a firewall, the amount of information obtained from scanning is far less than if the test were undertaken from an insider perspective. After identifying hosts on the network that can be reached from outside, testers attempt to compromise one of the hosts. If successful, this access may then be used to compromise other hosts that are not generally accessible from

---

[20] If given a list of authorized IP addresses to use as targets, assessors should verify that all public addresses (i.e., not private, unroutable addresses) are under the organization's purview before testing begins. Web sites that provide domain name registration information (e.g., WHOIS) can be used to determine owners of address spaces.

outside the network. Penetration testing is an iterative process that leverages minimal access to gain greater access.

Insider scenarios simulate the actions of a malicious insider. An internal penetration test is similar to an external test, except that the testers are on the internal network (i.e., behind the firewall) and have been granted some level of access to the network or specific network systems. Using this access, the penetration testers try to gain a greater level of access to the network and its systems through privilege escalation. Testers are provided with network information that someone with their level of access would normally have—generally as a standard employee, although depending on the goals of the test it could instead be information that a system or network administrator might possess.

Penetration testing is important for determining the vulnerability of an organization's network and the level of damage that can occur if the network is compromised. It is important to be aware that depending on an organization's policies, testers may be prohibited from using particular tools or techniques or may be limited to using them only during certain times of the day or days of the week. Penetration testing also poses a high risk to the organization's networks and systems because it uses real exploits and attacks against production systems and data. Because of its high cost and potential impact, penetration testing of an organization's network and systems on an annual basis may be sufficient. Also, penetration testing can be designed to stop when the tester reaches a point when an additional action will cause damage. The results of penetration testing should be taken seriously, and any vulnerabilities discovered should be mitigated. Results, when available, should be presented to the organization's managers. Organizations should consider conducting less labor-intensive testing activities on a regular basis to ensure that they are maintaining their required security posture. A well-designed program of regularly scheduled network and vulnerability scanning, interspersed with periodic penetration testing, can help prevent many types of attacks and reduce the potential impact of successful ones.

5.3   Social Engineering

Social engineering is an attempt to trick someone into revealing information (e.g., a password) that can be used to attack systems or networks. It is used to test the human element and user awareness of security, and can reveal weaknesses in user behavior—such as failing to follow standard procedures. Social engineering can be performed through many means, including analog (e.g., conversations conducted in person or over the telephone) and digital (e.g., e-mail, instant messaging). One form of digital social engineering is known as *phishing*, where attackers attempt to steal information such as credit card numbers, Social Security numbers, user IDs, and passwords. Phishing uses authentic-looking emails to request information or direct users to a bogus Web site to collect information. Other examples of digital social engineering include crafting fraudulent e-mails and sending attachments that could mimic worm activity.

Social engineering may be used to target specific high-value individuals or groups in the organization, such as executives, or may have a broad target set. Specific targets may be identified when the organization knows of an existing threat or feels that the loss of information from a person or specific group of persons could have a significant impact. For example, phishing attacks can be targeted based on publicly available information about specific individuals (e.g., titles, areas of interest). Individual targeting can lead to embarrassment for those individuals if testers successfully elicit information or gain access. It is important that the results of social engineering testing are used to improve the security of the organization and not to single out individuals. Testers should produce a detailed final report that identifies both successful and unsuccessful tactics used. This level of detail will help organizations to tailor their security awareness training programs.

5.4   Summary

Each information security testing technique has its own strengths and weaknesses. Table 5-1 compares the range of testing techniques discussed in Section 5.

Table 5-1. Target Vulnerability Validation Techniques

Technique	Capabilities
Password Cracking	• Identifies weak passwords and password policies
Penetration Testing	• Tests security using the same methodologies and tools that attackers employ • Verifies vulnerabilities • Demonstrates how vulnerabilities can be exploited iteratively to gain greater access
Social Engineering	• Allows testing of both procedures and the human element (user awareness)

Risks are associated with all techniques and technique combinations. To ensure that each technique is executed safely and accurately, testers should have a specific baseline skill set. Table 5-2 provides guidance on the minimum skill sets needed for testing techniques presented in this guide.

Table 5-2. Security Testing Knowledge, Skills, and Abilities

Technique	Baseline Skill Set
Password Cracking	Knowledge of secure password composition and password storage for operating systems; ability to use automated cracking tools
Penetration Testing	Extensive TCP/IP, networking, and OS knowledge; advanced knowledge of network and system vulnerabilities and exploits; knowledge of techniques to evade security detection
Social Engineering	Ability to influence and persuade people; ability to remain composed under pressure

6.   Security Assessment Planning

Proper planning is critical to a successful security assessment. This section provides guidance on creating an assessment policy, prioritizing and scheduling assessments, selecting the appropriate assessment approach, and addressing logistical considerations. It also provides recommendations for developing an assessment plan and outlines assessment-related legal considerations that organizations may need to address.

6.1   Developing a Security Assessment Policy

Organizations should develop an information security assessment policy to provide direction and guidance for their security assessments. This policy should identify security assessment requirements, and hold accountable those individuals responsible for ensuring that assessments comply with the requirements. It should address:

- Organizational requirements with which assessments must comply

- Appropriate roles and responsibilities (at a minimum, for those individuals approving and executing assessments)

- Adherence to established methodology

- Assessment frequency

- Documentation requirements, such as assessment plans and assessment results.

Once developed and approved by the appropriate senior officials, the policy should be disseminated to the appropriate staff—which might include the offices of the Chief Information Officer (CIO), Chief Information Security Officer (CISO), and Chief Technology Officer (CTO). Leadership should also communicate the policy to any third parties who are to conduct assessments.

It is recommended that organizations review their assessment policy at least annually, and whenever there are new assessment-related requirements. These reviews will determine the policy's continued applicability, address any necessary modifications, and provide opportunities for incorporating lessons learned.

6.2   Prioritizing and Scheduling Assessments

As part of planning, organizations should decide which systems should undergo technical security assessments and how often these assessments should be done. This prioritization is based on system categorization, expected benefits, scheduling requirements, and applicable regulations where assessment is a requirement. A good starting point is to evaluate system categorization and associated requirements for security assessment. Here, an evaluation of the system's impact rating (e.g., low, moderate, high)[21] and security assessment status (e.g., when was an assessment last conducted) is necessary to determine a schedule for moving forward. For instance, organizations should generally assess a high-impact system before a moderate-impact system—but a moderate-impact system that is overdue may need to be evaluated before a high-impact system whose last security assessment is still within the acceptable

---

[21]   FIPS PUB 199, *Standards for Security Categorization of Federal Information and Information Systems*, provides standards for determining the security category of an organization's information systems which can be helpful in developing a priority ranking of those systems for testing purposes. FIPS PUB 199 is available for download from http://csrc.nist.gov/publications/PubsFIPS.html.

timeframe. As part of continuous monitoring,[22] a number of NIST SP 800-53 security controls must also be constantly tested.[23]

Assessment frequency is often driven by an organization's requirements to demonstrate compliance with specific regulations or policies. For example, FISMA requires periodic testing depending on risk, to be done at least annually. NIST SPs 800-53 and 800-53A provide organizations with recommendations regarding the frequency of conducting security assessments. Since an assessment provides a snapshot of security at a given point in time, organizations may choose to require more frequent assessments.

Important technical considerations can also help determine testing frequency. For example, if a system is believed to have several weaknesses, testing might be conducted sooner to confirm the presence of the weaknesses—or delayed until the weaknesses have been mitigated, to confirm they have been resolved. The timing used depends on the testing objective. Another consideration is whether any system or network activities required by the testing may impact the functionality or security of the environment— for example, if a major upgrade is about to be conducted, testing might be delayed until the upgrade has been completed. Another example of a technical consideration is when an organization wants to identify rogue devices on wired networks. This could be accomplished using one or more techniques, such as performing network discovery through passive sniffing or active scanning, or reviewing data collected by network management software, network intrusion detection sensors, or other devices that routinely monitor network activity. If these monitoring devices are able to generate alerts as soon as a new, potentially rogue device is observed on the network, there may be little or no need to perform periodic testing for rogue devices because effective testing is continuously being performed.

Organizations also need to carefully consider resource availability. Resources should first be identified for high-priority systems, after which lower-priority systems may be tested with less frequency and in descending order. If a gap exists between required and available resources, the organization may need to allocate additional resources and consider reducing the scope of its planned assessments. Examples of scoping elements that may be relevant include:

■ The size of what is being assessed, in terms of number of components (e.g., single database, all user systems, or entire architecture) and network size (e.g., Local Area Network [LAN] or Wide Area Network [WAN], number of network locations that a tester will need to physically plug into for testing).

■ The complexity of what is being assessed. More heterogeneous environments generally require larger amounts of resources because more diverse skill sets and tools are needed.

■ The feasibility of using a sample for assessment, along with the sample size and its makeup. For example, it may be much more efficient—and nearly as effective—to port scan a small sample of hosts rather than thousands of hosts, especially if the hosts are managed and similarly configured.

■ The level of resources needed to conduct specific testing or examination techniques. For example, it could take many hours for a skilled assessor to review a system's complete security documentation.

---

[22]   NIST SP 800-37, *Guide for the Security Certification and Accreditation of Federal Information Systems,* Section 3.4, provides guidance on the continuous monitoring phase of the accreditation process. See http://csrc.nist.gov/publications/PubsSPs.html.

[23]   Continuous monitoring activities include configuration management and control of information system components, security impact analyses of changes to the system, ongoing assessment of security controls, and status reporting. NIST SP 800-53 http://csrc.nist.gov/publications/PubsSPs.html provides additional guidance.

■ The level of human interaction required. For instance, if assessors are to work in tandem with IT staff, this may serve as a form of training for the IT staff but will likely increase the time needed to complete the assessment when compared to the time needed by assessors and IT staff working independently.

6.3 Selecting and Customizing Techniques

There are many factors to consider when determining which technical testing and examination techniques should be used for a particular assessment. An organization should first determine its assessment objectives, such as focusing on verifying compliance with a particular mandate, verifying a system's security as part of certification and accreditation (C&A) activities, identifying exploitable vulnerabilities in a group of systems, or evaluating intrusion detection system and incident handling procedure performance. Next, the organization should select the classes of techniques (e.g., review, target identification and analysis, target vulnerability validation) to be used to obtain information that supports those objectives, and specific techniques within each selected class. For some testing techniques, the organization must also determine the assessors' viewpoint (e.g., internal versus external, covert versus overt) and select corresponding techniques.

Since in most cases more than one technique can be used to meet an assessment objective, organizations need to determine which techniques are best for each case. As discussed in Section 6.2, one important consideration is resources—some techniques may cost substantially more than others to use because of the types of tools required and the number of hours of staff time needed. Some techniques may also take too long to perform—if there is a short timeframe for conducting an assessment, less extensive or resource-intensive techniques may be needed, such as performing vulnerability scanning rather than a penetration test. Skills are another important factor in technique selection—for example, an organization may not have assessors on staff with the appropriate skill sets to use certain specialized techniques.

Organizations should also carefully consider risk when selecting testing techniques. Some techniques, such as penetration testing, could lead to loss of system availability or exposure of sensitive data. In some cases, organizations should consider whether testing should be performed on production systems or similarly configured non-production systems, if such alternate systems are available, or restrict the use of certain techniques to off-hours so as to minimize impact to operations. Factors to evaluate when making such decisions include:

■ The possible impact to the production systems. For example, if a particular test technique is likely to cause a denial of service, it should probably be used against a non-production system.

■ The presence of sensitive personally identifiable information (PII). If testing could expose sensitive PII—such as Social Security numbers (SSN) or credit card information—to individuals who are not authorized to have access, organizations should consider performing their testing on a non-production system with a false version of the PII (e.g., test data instead of actual PII).

■ How similarly the production and non-production systems can be configured. In practice, there are usually inconsistencies between the test and production environments, which can result in missed vulnerabilities if non-production systems are used.

Organizations often use a combination of techniques to achieve an in-depth security assessment while maintaining an acceptable level of risk to systems and networks. As mentioned in Section 2, non-technical techniques may be used instead of or in addition to technical techniques; many assessments use a combination of non-technical and technical techniques.

The following examples show how multiple technical techniques can complement one another and how selection of techniques can relate to risk concerns. These examples are intended as illustrations rather than as recommended combinations of techniques for organizations' assessments. Each case is different, and organizations should evaluate the requirements and objectives of each assessment when determining an appropriate combination of techniques.

■ Identify technical weaknesses in a system's security architecture and security configuration while minimizing risk from the assessment itself.

- **Step 1. Documentation Review.** Identify policy and procedure weaknesses and security architecture flaws.

- **Step 2. Ruleset and Security Configuration Review.** Identify deviations from organizational security policies in the forms of the system's network security architecture and system security flaws.

- **Step 3. Wireless Scanning.** Identify rogue wireless devices within proximity of the system, and additional security architecture weaknesses related to the wireless networks used by the system.

- **Step 4. Network Discovery and Vulnerability Scanning.** Identify all active hosts within the system and their known vulnerabilities.

■ Identify and validate technical weaknesses in a system's security architecture and security configuration—validation will include attempts to exploit selected vulnerabilities.

- **Step 1. Ruleset and Security Configuration Review.** Identify deviations from organizational security policies in the forms of the system's network security architecture and system security flaws.

- **Step 2. Network Discovery and Vulnerability Scanning.** Identify all active hosts within the system and their known vulnerabilities.

- Step 3. Penetration Test with Social Engineering. Validate vulnerabilities in the system.

■ Identify and validate technical weaknesses in a system's security architecture and security configuration from an external attacker's viewpoint—validation will include attempting to exploit some or all vulnerabilities. Evaluate the effectiveness of the organization's audit capabilities for attacks against the system.

- **Step 1. External Penetration Testing.** Perform external network discovery, port scanning, vulnerability scanning, and attacks to identify and validate system vulnerabilities.

- **Step 2. Log Review.** Review security control audit logs for the system to determine their effectiveness in capturing information relating to external penetration testing activities.

6.4   Assessment Logistics

Addressing logistics for technical assessments includes identifying all resources required for conducting the assessment; the environment from which to test; and required hardware and software testing tools. These are addressed in the subsections below.

In addition to the standard logistical requirements discussed below, it is equally important to identify logistical requirements for each test during the planning phase. Depending on the scope and the environment, individual tests may have additional logistical requirements such as submitting a visit request for an external test team, shipping equipment to a facility to enable testing, and planning for local or long-distance travel. These needs should be addressed on a case-by-case basis during the planning process.

6.4.1 Assessor Selection and Skills

Assessors conduct examinations and tests using technical methods and techniques, such as those described in this guide. Organizations should take care when selecting assessors, because properly vetted, skilled, and experienced assessors will lower the risks involved in conducting security tests. Because assessors may also require access to sensitive information on network architecture, security posture, and weaknesses, some organizations may require background checks or security clearances. Organizations should also be mindful of possible conflicts of interest, such as a single individual conducting a formal assessment and being responsible for addressing the findings of that assessment.

Many organizations have dedicated internal assessment teams. Depending on an organization's structure, size, location, and available resources, these teams may be divided by geographical location or centralized and deployed to various sites to conduct their assessments. Some teams address specific technical competencies, such as wireless security testing, while other teams can address many areas of security in varying levels of depth. For instance, a team may have among its members some individuals who are capable of reviewing a system configuration, others who can use automated assessment tools to identify known vulnerabilities, and still others who are able to actively exploit vulnerabilities to demonstrate ineffective security measures.

Assessors should have significant security and networking knowledge, including expertise in network security, firewalls, intrusion detection systems, operating systems, programming, and networking protocols (such as TCP/IP). A wide range of technical skill sets is required to conduct testing in an effective and efficient manner while ensuring minimal risk. Assessors should also be skilled in the specific types of techniques being executed, such as vulnerability identification and verification, security configuration, vulnerability management, and penetration testing. Operational experience is preferred to classroom or laboratory training. Allowing inexperienced or untrained staff to conduct technical tests can negatively affect an organization's systems and networks, potentially hindering its mission and damaging the credibility of its security program management office and assessors. It is also beneficial to have a technical writer or other individual on the team with strong technical writing skills. This helps the team to effectively convey the results of the assessment, particularly to less technical readers.

When assessments are performed by a team, the team leader facilitates the assessment process; demonstrates an understanding of the organization's environment and requirements; and (if applicable) eases communication between the assessors and the organization's security group. The team's leader should be selected based on overall technical knowledge and experience with the type of techniques being executed, and knowledge of the assets being assessed. Team leaders should also have strong communication, organization, planning, and conflict resolution skills.

The skills possessed by an assessment team should be balanced to provide a well-rounded view of the organization's security posture. For example, having an individual that specializes in perimeter defense is helpful, but having a team full of people that specialize in perimeter defense is likely to be redundant unless the testing's sole focus is to determine the perimeter's security posture. Ideally, a team is assembled based on the individual requirements of the examinations and tests being conducted. System characteristics may also be important—for instance, supervisory control and data acquisition (SCADA) systems have a number of unique components with which a traditional security assessor may not be familiar, reducing the assessor's ability to safely and adequately test the security posture of those systems.

In this type of case, one or more subject matter experts (SME) may be needed to augment the regular assessors. The SME may be an experienced security tester and system expert, or may be skilled only in the system being tested. Regardless, SMEs should be educated on the goals, objectives, approach, and process of the assessment—and should also be included in the planning process whenever possible because they may have critical knowledge to contribute.

Assessors need to remain abreast of new technology and the latest means by which an adversary may attack that technology. They should periodically refresh their knowledge base, reassess their methodology-updating techniques as appropriate, and update their tool kits. For example, attending technical training courses, performing hands-on testing in a test environment, or researching the latest vulnerabilities and exploits are just a few activities in which assessors should regularly engage. Assessors should also perform technical hands-on tests in operational environments on a regular basis to maintain and improve their skills.

Responsibilities of assessors include:

- Informing the appropriate parties—such as security officers, management, system administrators, and users—of security assessment activities

- Developing assessment plans with system managers, the Information Systems Security Officer (ISSO), and the CISO

- Executing examinations and tests, and collecting all relevant data

- Analyzing collected data and developing mitigation recommendations

- Conducting additional examinations and tests when needed to validate mitigation actions.

In some cases, engaging third parties (e.g., auditors, contractor support staff) to conduct the assessment offers an independent view and approach that internal assessors may not be able to provide. Organizations may also use third parties to provide specific subject matter expertise that is not available internally. While it can be beneficial to gain an external perspective on the security posture, giving outsiders access to an organization's systems can introduce additional risk. External entities should be properly vetted to ensure that they possess the necessary skills, experience, and integrity, and should be asked to assume some of the risk associated with the security assessment in that they may be responsible for damages incurred by the organization being assessed. External entities should also understand and comply with the organization's applicable policies and operational and security requirements.

In addition to those listed above, the responsibilities for external assessors include:

- Coordinating and communicating with the organization being assessed

- Ensuring that proper authority is granted, and maintaining a signed copy of the assessment plan to ensure all updates are documented

- Signing and abiding by any required nondisclosure agreements

- Properly protecting data in accordance with the organization's regulations, including handling, transmission, storage, and deletion of all collected data and resulting reports.

6.4.2 Location Selection

The environment in which assessors operate differs according to the techniques being used. For many types of tests, assessors can operate either onsite or offsite, with onsite testing defined as testing executed at the organization's location. Placing assessors offsite, however, may make the test more realistic (e.g., when applying the covert testing approach). For examinations, assessors are generally located onsite so they can easily access the organization's security documentation, logs, and other information. For assessments performed by third parties, the organization will need to determine the appropriate level of physical access (e.g., unrestricted, escorted). For technical assessments conducted from within the network—such as security configuration reviews and vulnerability scanning—assessors should be provided network access either onsite, through an encrypted virtual private network (VPN) tunnel, or via a dedicated connection from a trusted environment such as an approved test lab.[24]

Assessors may require different levels of access to the network depending on the tools that they use. Some tools require network or domain administrator privileges—if this is the case, organizations should create new administrator accounts for use during assessments. Each assessor should have his or her own account—administrator accounts should not be shared for any reason. This approach allows the organization to monitor these accounts, which will be disabled or deleted at the assessment's conclusion.

Technical assessments conducted from outside the network's perimeter can be executed following a number of scenarios, of which the most common are discussed here. The assessors' systems can be connected directly to a perimeter device (e.g., border router), which keeps the assessors within the organization's logical and physical boundaries. However, use of this location does not provide a true evaluation of the organization's security posture from an adversarial viewpoint. External tests can also be executed from a test lab with an Internet connection that is independent from the network of the organization being tested—and, if applicable, the organization conducting the testing (e.g., third-party assessors conducting the tests from their own facility).[25] Organizations conducting external tests may also choose to rent a server and an independent Internet connection. These services are provided by a variety of vendors, typically for a monthly fee. If a rented server is used, assessors should securely delete the data on the system and rebuild it before conducting a security test. Once testing is complete, the team should follow the guidelines provided in Section 7.4 for data handling.

When selecting a location for assessment activities, organizations should consider the inherent risks of using external locations. These typically offer less control over physical and logical access to external locations than internal locations, and may place assessment systems and data at a greater risk of compromise. Network traffic between the external location and the organization's facilities is also at greater risk of being monitored by unauthorized parties, which could expose security weaknesses detected by tests. There may also be issues with performing certain types of testing, such as penetration testing, over third-party networks—such tests may appear malicious in nature to security staff monitoring network usage, and may even violate the security policies of the network provider.

As previously discussed in Section 5, the location of the assessment systems may affect the results of certain types of tests. For example, if vulnerability scanning network traffic passes through a firewall, that firewall might inadvertently block portions of the traffic and prevent certain vulnerabilities from being detected. Also, intrusion detection and prevention systems and other security controls might block network traffic perceived as malicious in nature, such as certain types of tests. These problems are exacerbated when tests are run from an external location over a third-party network, in which case neither assessors nor the organization may have knowledge of or control over the security features interfering with test activities.

---

[24] Systems being tested may not be located on a production network, in which case the test team may need to be provided access to the non-production network used by those systems.

[25] Using an independent network is particularly advantageous if covert testing is being conducted. This can make it more difficult for the security staff to identify the source of the activity (i.e., the IP addresses are not associated with a test team or organization). Also, it prevents an inadvertent denial of service against legitimate users, which could occur if the security staff blocked access from the testers' IP address range in response to the testing activity.

6.4.3   Technical Tools and Resources Selection

Information systems built to execute a security assessment should meet the requirements of the specific type of assessment and its expected tools. For example, systems for document review should have applications installed to read documents, track vulnerabilities, and compose reports. Systems designed to execute tests such as vulnerability assessments and penetration testing are more complex in terms of system requirements and software tools. Systems for technical assessments can include servers, workstations, or laptops. Laptops are generally used by traveling assessors, and servers or workstations may be used if assessors are in a test lab or an onsite location. Assessors may also establish a network from which to execute techniques—this enables an environment that supports the centralized logging of activities and servers dedicated to activities that require increased processing power.

The requirements of test systems vary. A system that can handle the processing and memory requirements of all tools, operating systems, and virtual machines[26] (VM) should be used to lessen the likelihood of the system crashing during a test. A crash could cause that component of the test to need to be redone, data to be lost, and test systems to be rebuilt. Processing power and memory requirements are driven by both the tools used and the speed with which the test team expects to process certain components. For example, password cracking generally requires increased processing power and memory, so test teams may wish to have a dedicated password-cracking server. A dedicated system will allow the team to execute other test objectives during the password-cracking process. Hard drive requirements will depend on the expected amount of data collected during a test. In the event that long-term storage of the data is required, a storage method (e.g., independent system or removable media) should be identified and procured as appropriate.

Tools used by the test team will vary depending on the individual test scope, but the team should have a core set of tools that it uses and keeps up to date. Depending on the engagement and organization, a team may use a combination of tools developed in-house, open source tools, and/or commercial or government off-the-shelf (GOTS) tools. Tools should be obtained from well-established sources. Some organizations may also have specific tools they require or encourage teams to use—for example, an organization may purchase a license for a product that all its test teams can use. Many freeware tools are available as well. Appendix A lists common tools, and describes the purpose of and how it can be obtained. Organizations should take care to evaluate each tool before using it in a test—this process could range from downloading the tool from a trusted site to conducting an in-depth code review to ensure that the tool does not contain malicious code.

Often, tools will determine the operating system required to execute the testing—including the need for multiple operating systems. Systems may be configured a variety of ways, including single OS, single OS with VM images, and dual-boot systems. An example of a dual-boot system is a system that can be booted to either a version of Microsoft Windows or a version of Linux such as Red Hat, Mandrake, or SuSE. A dual-boot system allows a tester to use two operating systems from a single machine, but this can be inconvenient because the tester needs to reboot the system to switch between each OS and its tools.

Another more popular and functional option is to use VMs. Many testing tools require a specific operating system, and VMs allow testers to use a wider variety of tools more easily because they allow testers to switch from one OS to another without rebooting the system—enabling them to run multiple operating systems simultaneously. This has several possible benefits, including logging, documentation

---

[26] A virtual machine (VM) is software that allows a single host to run one or more guest operating systems. These operating systems do not interact and are not aware of each other. A virtual machine monitor is the piece of software that controls communication between the physical hardware and the individual VMs.

capabilities, and executing simultaneous tests. Since the system hosting the VM supports two or more operating systems at once, test systems running VMs require greater processing power and memory.

Testers should be knowledgeable, experienced, and comfortable using all operating systems found on the test system because system modifications are frequently required to operate specific tools or system capabilities successfully. For example, if the test team is using Red Hat Linux to conduct a wireless security test, the team will need to be familiar with installing and configuring wireless network cards because the steps for doing so may not be obvious to a Red Hat Linux novice.

Regardless of the system installation method used, organizations conducting security tests should develop and maintain a baseline image from which to conduct their tests. An image provides a standardized toolkit for the team to use, and enables rapid deployment of a team. The baseline image should consist of the operating system, drivers, requisite system and security configurations, applications, and tools to conduct testing, including mechanisms for automatically logging assessor actions (e.g., commands issued). Full system images are often hardware-dependent, so installing an image on another system with different hardware (e.g., video cards) requires the test team to modify the image—which involves specific skills and is time-consuming. VM images are more versatile and do not carry the same hardware restrictions as full system images, making them a more favorable option for test teams. Multifunction teams—such as those with the skills to conduct wireless scans, application testing, vulnerability assessments, and penetration tests—may have one image that contains the tools required to execute all test types or multiple images for various techniques. Using one image is generally preferable, as retaining multiple images requires additional maintenance.

The VM image should be updated periodically to ensure that only the latest tools and versions are being used. During this update period, the team should confirm tool functionality and identify—with documentation as appropriate—any changes in the functionality or use. Updating tools that discover vulnerabilities (e.g., vulnerability scanners) before each test helps ensure that recently discovered vulnerabilities are part of the testing. In addition to maintaining their existing toolset, the team should periodically assess its toolkit to identify obsolete tools to be removed and new tools that should be added.

Before using test systems in a security test, the test team should apply the latest security patches and enable only the services needed for connectivity and testing. This recommendation applies to all operating systems that may be used for testing, including those in VMs. The organization's security group may validate that test systems are compliant with the organization's security requirements and approved for testing before connecting these systems to the network. Validation can be done via the same systems used for technical tests such as vulnerability scans. Test systems may not meet all of the organization's security requirements because of the requirements of the tools used for testing—for example, some security controls may interfere with tool operation because they attempt to stop scans or attacks performed using those tools. In such cases, assessors may need to disable these security controls when the tools are in use.

Traveling teams should maintain a flyaway kit that includes systems, images, additional tools, cables, projectors, and other equipment that a team may need when performing testing at other locations. If an organization uses an external test team, this team should not use the organization's resources unless required to do so. If the organization does not authorize external systems to be connected to its network, the external test team will need to either install all required tools onto an approved client system or bring a bootable system emulation capability such as a live CD.[27] Appendix A provides examples of two live

---

[27] A live CD is a fully functioning operating system environment that is contained on a bootable CD. This technology does not require the user to load anything (e.g., software, drivers, etc) onto the system.

CD distributions. If tools are directly installed onto a client system, the test team should ensure that the tools and any files that they generate are removed from the system when testing is done.

6.5   Assessment Plan Development

An assessment plan provides structure and accountability by documenting the activities planned for an assessment, along with other related information. NIST SP 800-53A provides additional information on assessment plans, and addresses several distinct steps that assessors should consider in developing a plan. These steps are: (i) determining the type of security control assessment; (ii) determining the security controls and control enhancements to be included in the assessment; (iii) selecting the appropriate assessment procedures to be used during the assessment based on security controls and control enhancements in the system security plan; (iv) tailoring the selected assessment procedures for the information system impact level and organization's operating environment; (v) developing additional assessment procedures, if necessary, to address other security controls and control enhancements; (vi) developing a strategy to apply the extended assessment procedure; (vii) optimizing assessment procedures to reduce duplication of effort and provide cost-effective assessment solutions; and (vi) finalizing the assessment plan and obtaining the approvals needed for its execution..

Each assessment should be addressed in an assessment plan, regardless of the scope, level of intrusiveness, or party performing the test (i.e., internal, third party).[28] This plan provides the rules and boundaries to which assessors must adhere, and protects the organization by reducing the risk of an incident such as accidental system disruption or the inadvertent disclosure of sensitive information. Assessment plans also protect the test team by ensuring that the organization's management understands and agrees to the assessment's scope, activities, and limitations. Development of the assessment plan should be a collaborative process between the assessors and key members of the organization's security group.

The assessment plan should answer these basic questions:

- What is the scope of the assessment?

- Who is authorized to conduct the assessment?

- What are the assessment's logistics?

- How should sensitive data be handled?

- What should occur in the event of an incident?

The assessment plan should identify which systems and networks are authorized to be examined and tested. This can be done by providing the number of systems and the IP addresses or address ranges that they use. The plan should also list specific systems—at a minimum by IP address and preferably also by system name—that are not authorized to be examined or tested. For example, if an organization's payroll database is deemed too mission-critical for a particular type of testing, the system name and IP address should be included in the assessment plan's exclusion list. If the organization does not control part or all of its network, such as having a portion of its systems housed on a third party's network, the owner of the other network usually must also consent in writing to the assessment plan. A similar situation involves

---

[28]   In addition to an assessment plan, it may be useful to develop a shorter document (a one- or two-page memorandum) that assessors can present to parties in the organization (e.g., users or system owners) as authorization to gain access to particular systems. The document should describe allowable and unallowable activities, authorized and unauthorized systems, the acceptable level of cooperation to be provided by users, and a point of contact in the organization's security group that users can contact for more information.

systems that are shared by organizations, such as a system using virtual machine technology to provide services to multiple organizations. By signing the assessment plan, all parties acknowledge and approve of the assessment.

Besides determining which systems are authorized for assessment, the assessment plan should also detail the type and level of the testing permitted. For example, if the organization desires a vulnerability assessment, the assessment plan should provide information on activities authorized to be performed on the target network—such as port and service identification, vulnerability scanning, security configuration review, and password cracking—with enough detail included to describe the type of testing, approach, and tools. For example, if password cracking will be used, the method through which the passwords will be obtained (e.g., sniffed off the network or copied from the OS password file) should be included in the assessment plan. The plan should also explicitly state any activities that are prohibited—for example, file creation and modification—in a way that leaves no room for interpretation. If questions regarding scope and level of authorization arise during the course of an assessment, the assessors and the organization's identified point of contact should meet to discuss them.

The plan should also address the logistical details of the engagement—including the hours of operation for assessors; the clearance or background check level required; a call plan with current contact information, network and security operations centers, and the organization's main point of contact for the assessment; the physical location where assessment activities will originate; and the equipment and tools that will be used to conduct the assessment. Any requirements to inform parent organizations, law enforcement, and a computer incident response team (CIRT) should be identified in the assessment plan. In addition, the person responsible for informing the organizations of the pending security assessment should be identified. In the case of covert or other unannounced testing, the assessment plan should also define how test activity detected and reported by the organization's security staff, CIRT, and others should be handled—including as the escalation processes to be followed. The primary purpose for this is to ensure that assessment activity does not trigger reporting of security breaches to external parties, such as external incident response teams.

IP addresses of the machines from which assessment activities will be conducted should be identified in the assessment plan to enable administrators to differentiate assessment activities such as penetration testing attacks from actual malicious attacks. If appropriate for the goals of the assessment, security administrators can configure intrusion detection systems and other security monitoring devices to ignore activity generated by these IP addresses during testing.

Data handling requirements should be addressed in the assessment plan, including:

- Storage of organizational data during the assessment on the assessors' systems, including physical security of the systems, passwords, and data encryption

- Data storage upon conclusion of the assessment, to meet long-term storage requirements or vulnerability tracking

- Transmission of data during or after the assessment across internal or external networks (e.g., the Internet)

- Removal of data from systems upon conclusion of the assessment—in particular, for third-party assessments that include references to specific requirements set forth by the governing organization's policies or procedures.

Finally, the assessment plan should provide specific guidance on incident handling in the event that assessors cause or uncover an incident during the course of the assessment. This section of the plan should define the term *incident* and provide guidelines for determining whether or not an incident has occurred. The plan should identify specific primary and alternate points of contact for the assessors, generally the assessment team leader and assistant team leader, and the organization's security group. Guidelines should be included that clearly state actions to be taken by both the assessors and the organization's security group upon determination that an incident has occurred. For example, if the assessors discover an actual intruder or an intruder's footprints within the network, should testing stop? If so, when can testing recommence—and by whose authority? The assessment plan should provide clear-cut instructions on what actions assessors should take in these situations.

Some assessments use ROE in addition to or instead of an assessment plan. The ROE contains the same information in an assessment plan, and also addresses testing activities that are usually prohibited by the organization. For example, some activities that are often performed during penetration testing, such as issuing attacks to compromise systems, are usually prohibited by an organization's policies. The ROE provides authorization for the assessors to conduct such activities as part of the assessment process. Appendix B provides a sample template for an ROE.

Each organization should determine when assessment plans and/or ROEs should be used. Organizations should also consider developing central assessment plans, or ROE templates or partial drafts, and requiring their use to promote consistency.

6.6 Legal Considerations

An evaluation of potential legal concerns for an assessment should be addressed before the assessment begins. While the involvement of legal advisors is at the discretion of the organization, it is recommended that they always be involved for intrusive tests such as penetration testing. If an organization authorizes an external entity to conduct an assessment, the legal departments of each organization may be involved. These departments may assist in reviewing the assessment plan and providing indemnity or limitation of liability clauses into contracts that govern security assessments— particularly for types of tests that are deemed intrusive. The legal department may also require external entities to sign nondisclosure agreements that prohibit assessors from disclosing any sensitive, proprietary, or otherwise restricted information to unapproved entities.

The legal department should also address any privacy concerns that the organization may have. Most organizations have warning banners or signed user agreements that disclose their systems are monitored, warning that individuals consent to monitoring by their use of the system. However, not all organizations have these in place, and the legal department should address potential privacy violations before the assessment begins. In addition, captured data may include sensitive data that does not belong to the organization—or personal employee data, which may create privacy concerns. Assessors should be aware of these risks and conduct packet captures that follow any requirements set forth by the legal department. The legal department may also determine data handling requirements to ensure data confidentiality (e.g., vulnerabilities).

6.7 Summary

Information security assessment is a complex activity because of organizational requirements, the number and type of systems within an organization, the technical techniques to be used, and the logistics associated with assessments. Security assessments can be simplified and associated risks reduced through an established, repeatable planning process. Accurate and timely planning of a security assessment can also ensure that all factors necessary for assessment success are taken into account.

The core activities involved in planning for an assessment include:

■ **Developing a security assessment policy.** Organizations should develop an information security assessment policy to provide direction and guidance for their security assessments. This policy should identify security assessment requirements and hold accountable those individuals responsible for ensuring that assessments comply with the requirements. The approved policy should be disseminated to the appropriate staff, as well as third parties who are to conduct assessments for the organization. The policy should be reviewed at least annually and whenever there are new assessment-related requirements.

■ **Prioritizing and scheduling assessments.** Organizations should decide which systems should undergo assessments and how often these assessments should be done. This prioritization is based on system categorization, expected benefits, scheduling requirements, applicable regulations where assessment is a requirement, and resource availability. Technical considerations can also help determine assessment frequency, such as waiting until known weaknesses are corrected or a planned upgrade to the system is performed before conducting testing.

■ **Selecting and customizing technical testing and examination techniques.** There are many factors for organizations to consider when determining which techniques should be used for a particular assessment. Factors include the assessment objectives, the classes of techniques that can obtain information to support those objectives, and the appropriate techniques within each class. Some techniques also require the organization to determine the assessors' viewpoint (e.g., internal versus external) so that corresponding techniques can be selected.

■ **Determining the logistics of the assessment.** This includes identifying all required resources, including the assessment team; selecting environments and locations from which to perform the assessment; and acquiring and configuring all necessary technical tools.

■ **Developing the assessment plan.** The assessment plan documents the activities planned for an assessment and other related information. A plan should be developed for every assessment to provide the rules and boundaries to which assessors must adhere. The plan should identify the systems and networks to be assessed, the type and level of testing permitted, logistical details of the assessment, data handling requirements, and guidance for incident handling.

■ **Addressing any legal considerations.** Organizations should evaluate potential legal concerns before commencing an assessment, particularly if the assessment involves intrusive tests (e.g., penetration testing) or if the assessment is to be performed by an external entity. Legal departments may review the assessment plan, address privacy concerns, and perform other functions in support of assessment planning.

7. Security Assessment Execution

During execution of the security assessment, vulnerabilities are identified by the methods and techniques decided upon in the planning phase and identified in the assessment plan or ROE. It is critical that the assessment be conducted in accordance with the plan or ROE—and the purpose of this section is to highlight key points for assessors to consider throughout the execution phase. For example, proper coordination throughout the assessment facilitates the assessment process and reduces the possibility of associated risks. Key considerations such as incident handling and the challenges organizations face when conducting assessments are also highlighted. This section also discusses the analysis process, and provides recommendations for the collection, storage, transmission, and destruction of assessment-related data.

7.1 Coordination

Throughout an assessment, it is critical for assessors to coordinate with various entities in the organization. Coordination requirements are determined by the assessment plan or ROE and should be followed accordingly. Proper coordination helps to ensure that:

- Stakeholders are aware of the assessment schedule, activities, and potential impacts the assessment may have

- The assessment does not take place during upgrades, new technology integration, or other times when the system security is being altered (e.g., testing occurs during maintenance windows or periods of low utilization)

- Assessors are provided with required levels of access to the facility and systems, as appropriate

- Appropriate personnel such as the CIO, CISO, and ISSO are informed of any critical high-impact vulnerabilities as soon as they are discovered

- Appropriate individuals are informed (e.g., assessors, incident response team, senior management) in the event of an incident. Should this occur, it is recommended that activities cease until the incident is addressed and the assessors are given approval to resume their activities in accordance with the assessment plan or ROE. The extent to which assessment activities should be suspended varies based on the organization and the type of incident, but in many cases the only activities suspended are those involving the systems directly involved in the incident.

The level of coordination between assessors and the organization are driven primarily by the system and the assessment being conducted. Critical systems generally require more coordination to ensure system availability throughout the engagement, and assessment techniques pose varying levels of risk to the target system during execution. Techniques that fall in the review category have minimal risk; target identification and analysis category have moderate risk; and a high risk is associated with the target vulnerability validation category. For instance, a critical system undergoing penetration testing generally requires more coordination than would a document review of a critical system or a penetration test of a noncritical system. However, organizations may encounter circumstances where the reverse is true, and in such cases the level of coordination should be commensurate with requirements and organizational considerations. Assessors and other stakeholders—such as system owners—should remain vigilant during the execution of assessments. The level of access required by assessors will also drive coordination to ensure they have appropriate physical and system access (e.g., when testing the insider threat).

Assessors should be proactive in their communication with the appropriate parties in the organization. This communication can be maintained through periodic status meetings and daily or weekly reports. Meeting attendees and report recipients should be identified in the assessment plan or ROE, and may include the assessors, ISSO, CISO, and CIO. The frequency of status meetings and reports will be driven by the assessment's length and complexity. For example, for a one-month penetration test, status meetings may be held weekly with daily reports provided during the active testing phase (i.e., the period during which systems are being exploited). Meetings and reports should address activities completed to date, success rate, problems encountered, and critical findings/recommended remediation.

7.2   Assessing

As discussed in Section 6, the assessment plan or ROE provides guidelines for conducting the assessment. The plan or ROE should be followed unless specific permission to deviate has been obtained, normally in writing, from the original signatory or individual in command. It is critical that all assessors read and understand the plan or ROE. It is recommended that assessors periodically review the plan or ROE during the assessment—particularly in the case of activities in the target vulnerability validation category.

During an assessment, the organization's incident response team may detect an incident. This could be caused by the assessors' actions—or by a real adversary that happens to perform an attack while the assessment is in progress. Regardless, the incident response team or individual discovering the incident should follow the organization's normal escalation procedures, and assessors should follow the guidelines set forth by the assessment plan or ROE unless instructed otherwise. If the presence of an adversary is found during the assessment, it should immediately be reported to the appropriate individual and assessors should follow the protocol identified in the assessment plan or ROE. It is recommended that assessors stop assessing the systems involved in the incident while the organization carries out its response.

In addition to encountering new incidents or uncovering existing ones, assessors may face other technical, operational, and political challenges during an assessment. These can include:

- **Resistance.** Resistance to assessments can come from many sources within an organization, including system and network administrators and end users. Reasons may include fear of losing system or network availability, fear of being reprimanded, inconvenience, and resistance to change. Obtaining upper management approval and support will help resolve problems related to resistance, and incorporating security assessments into the organization's overall security policy will help establish a process that does not surprise administrators and users.

- **Lack of Realism.** In preparing for an assessment, users and administrators sometimes modify settings to make their systems more secure, resistant to attack, or more compliant with policies and other requirements. While this can be viewed as positive, changes made under these circumstances are generally only maintained for the duration of the assessment, after which the systems are returned to their previous configurations. Providing no advance notice of assessments to users and administrators helps to address this challenge. Many organizations perform occasional unannounced assessments to supplement their announced assessments.

- **Immediate Mitigation.** As security weaknesses are identified during an assessment, administrators may want to take immediate steps to mitigate them and expect assessors to quickly re-assess the system to confirm that the problems have been resolved. Although this desire for quick mitigation is admirable, assessors should communicate the importance of following the organization's change management policies and procedures.

- **Time.** Security assessment is often incorporated into development or deployment with little notice and narrow timeframes when it should actually be made a regular part of the development or deployment cycle. Time is also a challenge when testing critical systems and networks that are in production—if testing techniques have the potential to cause loss of availability or other problems, systems and networks may need to be tested off-hours. Assessors are often restricted to testing timeframes, while real attackers are not limited to such constraints.

- **Resources.** Security assessment faces the continual challenge of obtaining and maintaining adequate resources (e.g., a skilled test team and up-to-date hardware and software). It is suggested that organizations designate security assessment equipment—such as laptops and wireless cards—to be used solely for assessments.[29] If commercial assessment software is used, the purchase of continuous licenses and support contracts should be considered. Assessors should schedule time before the assessment begins to ensure that all assessment software is properly patched and up to date. If internal assessors are not available or do not meet assessment requirements, it may be a challenge to find dependable, trustworthy outside assessors. Organizations should seek a firm with an established methodology, proven processes, comparable and sufficient past performance, and experienced personnel. If an organization is using internal assessors, it should continue to recruit and train skilled assessors and offer other challenging opportunities within the organization where assessors can become involved to avoid burnout.

- **Evolving Technology.** Assessors need to stay up to date on tools and testing techniques. Budgets should allow for annual training classes and conferences where assessors can update and refresh their skills.

- **Operational Impact.** Although assessments are planned to prevent or limit operational impact, there is always a chance of accidental or unexpected complications. Every test conducted should be recorded with a timestamp, test type, tool used, commands, the IP address of testing equipment, etc. It is recommended that a logging script be used to capture all commands and keystrokes used during the testing process. Terminal and GUI tools exist that can record a tester's actions, and this type of recording can also assist in countering accusations that testing has negatively impacted operations and system performance. Because of the risk of operational impact, it is recommended that an established incident response plan be in place during testing.

7.3 Analysis

Although some analysis may be performed after an assessment has been completed (see Section 8.1), most analysis occurs during the assessment itself. The primary goals in conducting analysis are to identify false positives, categorize vulnerabilities, and determine the vulnerabilities' causes. Automated tools can produce a significant number of findings, but these findings often need to be validated to isolate false positives. Assessors may validate vulnerabilities by manually examining the vulnerable system or by using a second automated tool and comparing the results. Although this can be done quickly, these comparison tools can often produce similar results—including the same false positives. Manual examination typically provides more accurate results than comparing results from multiple tools, but it also has the potential to be time-consuming.

Organizations may choose to categorize their findings according to the security controls and control families in NIST SP 800-53, which organizes controls into families such as incident response and access control. This categorization may facilitate vulnerability analysis, remediation, and documentation.

---

[29] Organizations may want to disconnect their dedicated test equipment from networks when testing is not taking place.

While individual vulnerabilities need to be identified and resolved, identifying the root cause of vulnerabilities is key to improving the organization's overall security posture because a root cause can often be traced to program-level weaknesses. Some common root causes include:

- Insufficient patch management, such as failing to apply patches in a timely fashion or failing to apply patches to all vulnerable systems

- Insufficient threat management, including outdated antivirus signatures, ineffective spam filtering, and firewall rulesets that do not enforce the organization's security policy

- Lack of security baselines, such as inconsistent security configuration settings on similar systems

- Poor integration of security into the system development life cycle, such as missing or unsatisfied security requirements and vulnerabilities in organization-developed application code

- Security architecture weaknesses, such as security technologies not being properly integrated into the infrastructure (e.g., poor placement, insufficient coverage, or outdated technologies), or poor placement of systems that increases their risk of compromise

- Inadequate incident response procedures, such as delayed responses to penetration testing activities

- Inadequate training, both for end users (e.g., failure to recognize social engineering and phishing attacks, deployment of rogue wireless access points) and for network and system administrators (e.g., deployment of weakly secured systems, poor security maintenance)

- Lack of security policies or policy enforcement (e.g., open ports, active services, unsecured protocols, rogue hosts, weak passwords).

A useful resource to reference throughout the analysis phase is the NIST National Vulnerability Database (NVD)[30]. NVD is a database that contains information on Common Vulnerabilities and Exposures (CVE), a list of standardized names for known vulnerabilities. The NVD scores vulnerabilities with the Common Vulnerability Scoring System (CVSS) and provides additional information regarding the vulnerability and additional resources to reference for mitigation recommendations (e.g., vendor Web sites).

Another goal of analysis is to identify throughout the assessment any critical vulnerabilities that the organization needs to immediately address. For instance, if penetration testing exploits a vulnerability that allows assessors to gain administrator rights on a critical system, assessors should immediately notify the person identified in the assessment plan or ROE.

7.4   Data Handling

The method by which an organization's data is handled throughout the assessment is critical to ensuring protection of sensitive information—including system architecture, security configurations, and system vulnerabilities. Organizations should ensure proper documentation of requirements for data handling in the assessment plan or ROE, and adhere to their governing policies regarding the handling of system vulnerabilities. This section offers suggested methods for collecting, storing, and transmitting assessment data during an engagement, as well as for storing and destroying data once an assessment is complete.

---

[30]   The NVD website is http://nvd.nist.gov/.

7.4.1 Data Collection

Relevant information should be collected by the team throughout the assessment. This includes information related to the architecture and configuration of the networks being assessed, as well as information on assessor activities. Because this data is sensitive, it is important to handle it appropriately. Types of information the assessors might collect include:

- **Architecture and Configuration Data.** Assessment type and desired outcome will drive the data collected by the team, which may include but not be limited to system names, IP addresses, OS, physical and logical network positions, security configurations, and vulnerabilities.

- **Assessor Activities.** Assessors should keep a log that includes assessment system information and a step-by-step record of their activities. This provides an audit trail, and allows the organization to distinguish between the actions of assessors and true adversaries. The activity log can also be useful in developing the assessment results report.

Use of a keystroke logger on an assessor's system can create a step-by-step log of many tester actions, although it will not capture mouse clicks and certain other actions.[31] For automated tools, assessors can maintain the audit logs from each tool that is used. While assessors may choose to dump the output of the keystroke logger or tool audit log onto a separate system to create a centralized storage and auditing capability, an alternate manual approach is an activities log that tracks each command executed by assessors on the network. This approach is time-consuming for the assessors, and leaves room for error. If an activities log is used, it should include at a minimum the following information—date and time, assessor's name, assessment system identifier (i.e., IP or MAC), target system identifier (i.e., IP or MAC), tool used, command executed, and comments.

7.4.2 Data Storage

Secure storage of data collected during the assessment, including vulnerabilities, analysis results, and mitigation recommendations, is the assessors' responsibility. Inappropriate release of this information can damage the organization's reputation and increase the likelihood of exploitation. At a minimum, assessors should store the following information to be used for identifying, analyzing, and reporting on the security posture of the organization, and provide an audit trail of testing activities:

- Assessment plans and ROEs

- Documentation on system security configuration and network architecture

- Results from automated tools and other findings

- Assessment results report

- Corrective action plan or Plan of Action and Milestones (POA&M).

Many options exist for storing information on discovered vulnerabilities, such as keeping the findings in the format output by the tool that was used, or importing the findings into a database.[32] Most vulnerability scanning tools have report formats that list the system, vulnerabilities, and recommended mitigation

---

[31] A keystroke logger records every keystroke made by the user of the system, and places it into a log. This level of recording provides assessors with a method to track each action on the network—and allows the organization being assessed to see exactly what the assessors executed on the network, when it occurred, and which system conducted the test. In addition, this type of recording provides assessors with documentation that they were not the cause of malfunctioning or compromise of a network system.

[32] Storing vulnerability information can also be helpful for performing historical comparisons.

techniques. This may be an acceptable approach if the assessment is small in scope (e.g., only uses one tool). For more in-depth assessments, larger organizations, or assessments that use multiple tools or approaches, a more robust and collaborative storage method—such as a spreadsheet or database—can be developed. Although functionality is limited, a spreadsheet may be appropriate for individual examinations or tests, as it is easy to use, usually quick to develop, and can accommodate a number of tools that can output findings in a compatible format. For complex examinations or tests with multiple technical approaches, assessment actions that regularly recur, or situations with a need to correlate data easily, developing a database may be beneficial.

Organizations should ensure the secure storage of all sensitive assessment data, such as the assessment plan or ROE, raw vulnerability data, and assessment reports. In the hands of an adversary, information regarding network architecture, system configuration, security controls, and specific system vulnerabilities would provide a blueprint and roadmap for exploiting the organization's information systems. Organizations may choose to store this data on removable media, or on an information system that could be accessed as needed. The removable media or system designed to store this information should be isolated physically or logically from day-to-day network resources. Access to this system and the information it contains should be limited to those individuals whose access is needed to fulfill roles and responsibilities. This data is also recommended to be encrypted in compliance with FIPS 140-2 to ensure that it remains secure.

Retention requirements for security assessments data vary and may not be explicitly stated for an organization, in which case retention requirements for the assessment should be specified in the assessment plan or ROE. Maintaining accurate records for an assessment provides an organization with an audit trail of its vulnerabilities and the remediation actions it has taken to mitigate identified risks. An audit trail maintained over time may allow organizations to evaluate the effectiveness of their information security program by conducting trend analyses of metrics involving vulnerability type, frequency of occurrence, mean time to remediation, etc.

Assessment systems—such as servers, laptops, or other mobile devices—should not be left unattended when storing sensitive data without the proper physical and logical security safeguards in place. For example, mobile systems should not be left in unlocked vehicles or in plain sight in locked vehicles, and mobile devices in hotel rooms should be secured by a cable lock, stored in a room safe, or physically secured by other means. In addition to these physical safeguards, assessors should ensure that the system is configured in a way that deters adversaries from compromising it. Assessors should take appropriate measures to ensure the integrity and confidentiality of data a system contains, and protect the system at a minimum with a strong password—and it is suggested that organizations consider using two-factor authentication.[33] In addition, all sensitive data on the system should be encrypted,[34] and an authentication mechanism separate from the system authentication should be used to restrict access to the encrypted information.

7.4.3   Data Transmission

It may be necessary to transmit assessment data, such as system configurations and vulnerabilities, over the network or Internet, and it is important to ensure the security of the data being transmitted to protect it from compromise. The assessment plan or ROE should address the requirements of, and process for, transmitting sensitive system information across the network or Internet. Secure data transmission methods include encrypting individual files containing sensitive information, encrypting communication

---

[33]   Two-factor authentication provides additional security by requiring two of the following three factors—something you know (e.g., password), something you have (e.g., security token), and something you are (e.g., retinal scan).

[34]   Such data should be encrypted in compliance with FIPS 140-2 to ensure that it remains secure.

channels using FIPS-compliant encryption (e.g., VPNs, Secure Sockets Layer [SSL] protocol), and providing information through delivered or mailed hard or soft copies.

7.4.4 Data Destruction

When assessment data is no longer needed, the assessment systems, hard copy documentation, and media should be appropriately sanitized. NIST SP 800-88, *Guidelines for Media Sanitization*[35] divides media sanitization into four categories:

- **Disposal:** the act of discarding media with no other sanitization considerations. This is most often done by recycling paper that contains nonconfidential information, but may also include other media.

- **Clearing:** a level of media sanitization that would protect information confidentiality against a robust keyboard attack. Simple deletion of items does not suffice for clearing. Clearing must keep information from being retrieved by data, disk, or file recovery utilities, and must be resistant to keystroke recovery attempts executed from standard input devices and data scavenging tools. Overwriting is an example of an acceptable method for clearing media.

- **Purging:** a media sanitization process that protects information confidentiality against a laboratory attack.[36] For some media, clearing media does not suffice for purging. Examples of alternatives to clearing media are executing the firmware Secure Erase command (for Advanced Technology Attachment [ATA] drives only) and degaussing[37].

- **Destruction:** physical obliteration of media to render it no longer usable for its intended purpose and making the data it contains no longer retrievable. Physical destruction is possible through a variety of methods, including disintegration, incineration, pulverizing, shredding, and melting.

Organizations should maintain a policy on their sanitization requirements for assessment systems. NIST SP 800-88 presents a decision-flow diagram to assist organizations in determining which sanitization method is most applicable for their circumstances. An assessment plan or ROE may also specify destruction requirements for particular tests.

Third-party assessors should ensure that they understand the organization's requirements for sanitization, as policy may differ between organizations and possibly among divisions within the same organization. For example, some organizations prohibit third-party assessors from having any access to assessment data once their final reports have been submitted. In such cases, a qualified individual from the organization being assessed should verify that appropriate sanitization measures have been carried out.

---

[35] NIST SP 800-88 is available at http://csrc.nist.gov/publications/PubsSPs.html.
[36] A laboratory attack would involve an attacker with the resources and knowledge to use nonstandard systems to conduct data recovery attempts on media outside the normal operating environment. This type of attack involves using signal processing equipment and specially trained personnel.
[37] Degaussing is exposing the magnetic media to a strong magnetic field to disrupt the recorded magnetic domains.

8. Post-Testing Activities

Following the execution phase—whose findings are expressed in terms of vulnerabilities—the organization should take steps to address the vulnerabilities that have been identified. This section presents ways that organizations can translate their findings into actions that will improve security. First, final analysis of the findings should be performed, and mitigation actions developed. Second, a report should be developed to present the recommendations. Lastly, the mitigation activities should be carried out. Many of the actions presented in this section may occur outside of the testing process itself—for example, as part of a risk assessment that utilizes testing results.

8.1 Mitigation Recommendations

As described in Section 7.3, most analysis occurs during the testing process. Final analysis, such as the development of overall conclusions, usually takes place after all testing activities have been completed and involves the development of mitigation recommendations. While identifying and categorizing vulnerabilities is important, a security test is much more valuable if it also results in a mitigation strategy being developed and implemented. Mitigation recommendations, including the outcome of the root cause analysis, should be developed for each finding. There may be both technical recommendations (e.g., applying a particular patch) and nontechnical recommendations that address the organization's processes (e.g., updating the patch management process). Examples of mitigation actions include policy, process, and procedure modifications; security architecture changes; deployment of new security technologies; and deployment of OS and application patches.

NIST SP 800-53 suggests mitigation recommendations for each security control. Organizations should compare potential mitigation actions against operational requirements to determine the actions that best balance functionality and security. Section 8.3 discusses the implementation of mitigation recommendations.

8.2 Reporting

Upon completion of analysis, a report should be generated that identifies system, network, and organizational vulnerabilities and their recommended mitigation actions. Security testing results can be used in the following ways:

- As a reference point for corrective action

- In defining mitigation activities to address identified vulnerabilities

- As a benchmark for tracking an organization's progress in meeting security requirements

- To assess the implementation status of system security requirements

- To conduct cost/benefit analysis for improvements to system security

- To enhance other life cycle activities, such as risk assessments, C&A, and process improvement efforts

- To meet reporting requirements, such as those of FISMA.

Security testing results should be documented and made available to the appropriate staff, which may include the CIO, CISO, and ISSO as well as appropriate program managers or system owners. Because a report may have multiple audiences, multiple report formats may be required to ensure that all are appropriately addressed. For example, organizations developing reports for FISMA compliance need to address FISMA requirements such as reporting on findings from evaluations, compliance with NIST standards, significant deficiencies, and planned remediation activities. Reports that will remain within the organization can be tailored for the appropriate audiences, such as program management, information management, security engineers, configuration management, or technical staff. Internal reports should include test methodology, test results, analysis, and POA&M.[38] A POA&M will ensure that individual vulnerabilities are addressed with specific, measurable, attainable, realistic, and tangible actions.

8.3 Remediation/Mitigation

The POA&M provides the program management office with the details and required actions needed to appropriately and acceptably mitigate risk. As a complement to the POA&M, organizations may consider developing a strategy or process for implementing the plan. Organizations should follow at least the four steps outlined below during their remediation implementation process—these will provide consistency and structure for security personnel and program managers.

The first step in the process is testing the remediation recommendation. Before implementing technical modifications to a production asset, testing should be done on test systems in an environment that replicates the network in which the mitigation action would be implemented. For example, before being pushed to the enterprise, patches should be installed on comparable systems in the test environment to determine if there are any negative implications. Such testing significantly reduces, but does not eliminate, the risk of a system reacting adversely to a technical modification.

Second, the POA&M should be coordinated through an organization's configuration control or configuration management board because the POA&M likely proposes changes to existing systems, networks, policy, or processes. Communicating POA&M changes both before deployment and upon completion ensures that the appropriate individuals are aware of the pending changes and their impact on environment, mission, and operations. At a minimum, the program manager or system owner should be contacted before executing any POA&M actions and should provide approval of the planned mitigation actions before they are implemented.

Obtaining management approval can be challenging. It may be beneficial to identify why it is needed (i.e., whether it is driven by policy or technology) and the positive impact that will be realized with the mitigation action (i.e., increased security posture or compliance). A cost/benefit analysis may also provide managers with a quantitative analysis of the increased savings to be realized by implementing the POA&M items. Additional benefits that may be communicated to senior management include decreased exposure, increased control of assets, decreased vulnerabilities, a proactive approach to security, and maintenance of compliance.

Third, mitigation actions are implemented and verified to ensure their appropriate and accurate implementation. Verification can take place by conducting an audit of the system, retesting the system and its components, and holding personnel accountable through documentation. A system audit provides technical verification of the changes that have been implemented on the system, and can be conducted by onsite security personnel or an external security test team. The audit team may use the mitigation strategy as a checklist for ensuring that each action is accomplished—also, retesting the system will validate that the mitigation actions have been completed. It is important to note that the test team will be able to verify its implementation only if a mirror copy of the original test is performed. As technology evolves,

---

[38] NIST SP 800-37 notes that a POA&M "describes the measures that have been implemented or planned: (i) to correct any deficiencies noted during the assessment of the security controls; and (ii) to reduce or eliminate known vulnerabilities in the information system. The plan of actions and milestones document identifies: (i) the tasks needing to be accomplished; (ii) the resources required to accomplish the elements of the plan; (iii) any milestones in meeting the tasks; and (iv) scheduled completion dates for the milestones."

additional vulnerabilities may be uncovered during follow-up security tests. An organization may also choose to verify implementation of the mitigation strategy through nontechnical means such as documentation. For example, it may be appropriate and cost-effective to hold the security personnel responsible for implementing the mitigation strategy accountable by requesting that they sign a document describing all of the accomplished actions. While this method is more cost-effective in the short term for an organization, there are risks posed by not technically verifying that changes have been implemented.

Last, as part of the implementation strategy, it is important to continuously update POA&Ms to identify activities that have been accomplished, partially accomplished, or are pending action by another individual or system. Ensuring that the POA&M is integrated into the organization's configuration management process will facilitate centralized tracking and management of changes to systems, policies, processes, and procedures, as well as provide an oversight mechanism that will address compliance requirements.

Appendix A—Live CD Distributions for Security Testing

Live distribution CDs focused on security testing are available to the public at no charge, and provide security testers with a live distribution OS that contains tools for security testing.[39] The OS distribution is loaded onto a CD-ROM, Universal Serial Bus (USB) drive, or other peripheral device. It is not installed onto a system, but is run directly from the device on which it is loaded—hence its designation as a "live" distribution. Two such distributions are BackTrack and Knoppix Security Tool Distribution (STD).

BackTrack[40] features a collection of over 300 security tools for network discovery, scanning and sniffing, password cracking, remote access testing, Bluetooth testing, computer forensics, and penetration testing. It offers user modularity, meaning that the user can customize distribution to include personal scripts or additional tools. BackTrack also includes tools to analyze Voice over Internet (VoIP) protocols such as the Session Initiation Protocol (SIP); tools such as Cisco Global Exploiter (CGE) and Cisco Torch that specifically target Cisco systems; and Metasploit, a vulnerability assessment tool. Recognizing the growing importance of application security testing, it also includes tools such as Peach, Fuzzer, and the Java tool, Paros Proxy. Table A-1 provides a sample of the tools available in BackTrack.[41]

Table A-1. BackTrack Toolkit Sample

Security Testing Technique	Security Testing Tool
Review	
Network Sniffing	Dsniff, Ettercap, Kismet, Mailsnarf, Msgsnarf, Ntop, Phoss, SinFP, SMB Sniffer, and Wireshark
File Integrity Checking	Autopsy, Foremost, RootkitHunter, and Sleuthkit
Target Identification and Analysis	
Application Security Testing	CIRT Fuzzer, Fuzzer 1.2, NetSed, Paros Proxy, and Peach
Network Discovery	Autonomous System Scanner, Ettercap, Firewalk, Netdiscover, Netenum, Netmask, Nmap, P0f, Tctrace, and Umit
Network Port and Service Identification	Amap, AutoScan, Netdiscover, Nmap, P0f, Umit, and UnicornScan
Vulnerability Scanning	Firewalk, GFI LANguard, Hydra, Metasploit, Nmap, Paros Proxy, Snort, and SuperScan
Wireless Scanning	Airsnarf, Airsnort, BdAddr, Bluesnarfer, Btscanner, FakeAP, GFI LANguard, Kismet, and WifiTAP
Target Vulnerability Validation	
Password Cracking	Hydra, John the Ripper, RainbowCrack, Rcrack, SIPcrack, SIPdump, TFTP-Brute, THC PPTP, VNCrack, and WebCrack
Remote Access Testing	IKEProbe, IKE-Scan, PSK-Crack, and VNC_bypauth
Penetration Testing	Driftnet, Dsniff, Ettercap, Kismet, Metasploit, Nmap, Ntop, SinFP, SMB Sniffer, and Wireshark

---

[39] Such toolkits do not necessarily include all the tools that would be needed for a particular test—in many cases, toolkits will need to be supplemented with additional tools.

[40] BackTrack is derived from two separate Linux live security-based distributions, WHAX and the Auditor Security Collection. Both were popular for their abundance of security tools and ease of use. Shortly after the creators of each distribution began to collaborate, they released the first non-beta version, renamed BackTrack, in May 2006. BackTrack quickly became and remains a favorite toolset among security professionals. BackTrack 3.0 is the version referenced for this publication.

[41] Many of the tools listed in Tables A-1 and A-2 could be listed for additional techniques, but for brevity they are not.

An older Linux live OS distribution and open source security toolset is Knoppix STD, which is based on Knoppix Linux. It was created by a security professional to assist with teaching security techniques to others. Knoppix STD was first released in May 2004 as Knoppix-STD 0.1 and has not been updated since. The lack of a newer version is due to its creator leaving the project. Version 0.1 is the version referred to for this publication. Before BackTrack, Knoppix STD was the benchmark security toolset and it remains widely used.

Similar to BackTrack, Knoppix STD enables network discovery, port and service identification, network sniffing, password cracking, forensics, and remote access testing. While there is some overlap between the distributions, there are some differences as well. Knoppix contains some tools that BackTrack does not, such as Netcat and Nessus; addresses technology areas such as cryptography; and offers more tools for computer forensics and sniffing. It does not provide Metasploit, and compared to BackTrack is weak on wireless security tools. Table A-2 provides a sample of the tools available on the Knoppix STD distribution.

Table A-2. Knoppix STD Toolkit Sample

Security Testing Technique	Security Testing Tool
Review	
Network Sniffing	Dsniff, Ettercap, Ethereal, Filesnarf, Kismet, Mailsnarf, Msgsnarf, Ngrep, Ntop, TCPdump, and Webspy
File Integrity Checking	Autopsy, Biew, Bsed, Coreography, Foremost, Hashdig, Rifiuti, and Sleuthkit
Target Identification and Analysis	
Application Security Testing	NetSed
Network Discovery	Cryptcat, Ettercap, Firewalk, Netcat, Nmap, and P0f
Network Port and Service Identification	Amap, Netcat, Nmap, and P0f
Vulnerability Scanning	Exodus, Firewalk, Nmap, and Snort
Wireless Scanning	Airsnarf, Airsnort, GPSdrive, Kismet, and MACchanger
Target Vulnerability Validation	
Password Cracking	Allwords2, chntpw, Cisilia, Djohn, Hydra, John the Ripper, and Rcrack
Remote Access Testing	Apache Server, IKE-Scan, Net-SNMP, SSHD, TFTPD, and VNC Server
Penetration Testing	Driftnet, Dsniff, Ethereal, Ettercap, Kismet, Nessus, Netcat, Ngrep, Nmap, Ntop, and TCPdump

Appendix B—Rules of Engagement Template

This template provides organizations with a starting point for developing their ROE.[42] Individual organizations may find it necessary to include information to supplement what is outlined here.

1. Introduction

1.1. Purpose

Identifies the purpose of the document as well as the organization being tested, the group conducting the testing (or, if an external entity, the organization engaged to conduct the testing), and the purpose of the security test.

1.2. Scope

Identifies test boundaries in terms of actions and expected outcomes.

1.3. Assumptions and Limitations

Identifies any assumptions made by the organization and the test team. These may relate to any aspect of the test to include the test team, installation of appropriate safeguards for test systems, etc.

1.4. Risks

Inherent risks exist when conducting information security tests—particularly in the case of intrusive tests. This section should identify these risks, as well as mitigation techniques and actions to be employed by the test team to reduce them.

1.5. Document Structure

Outlines the ROE's structure, and describes the content of each section.

2. Logistics

2.1. Personnel

Identifies by name all personnel assigned to the security testing task, as well as key personnel from the organization being tested. Should include a table with all points of contact for the test team, appropriate management personnel, and the incident response team. If applicable, security clearances or comparable background check details should also be provided.

2.2. Test Schedule

Details the schedule of testing, and includes information such as critical tests and milestones. This section should also address hours during which the testing will take place—for example, it may be prudent to conduct technical testing of an operational site during evening hours rather than during peak business periods.

---

[42] The structure of this template is intended to be illustrative. Organizations should organize their ROEs in whatever manner they choose.

2.3.   Test Site

Identifies the location or locations from which testing is authorized. If testing will occur on the organization's site, building and equipment access should be discussed. Physical access should cover requirements such as badges, escorts, and security personnel that the testers may encounter. Equipment access should address areas such as level of access (user or administrator) to the systems and/or network, and physical access to computer rooms or specific racks that these rooms contain. Areas to which the test team will not be given access should be identified here as well.

If testing will be conducted from a remote location such as a rented server farm or test lab, details of the test site architecture should be included in this section.

2.4.   Test Equipment

Identifies equipment that the test team will use to conduct the information security tests. This section should also identify the method of differentiating between the organization's systems and the systems conducting the testing—for example, if the test team's systems are identified by MAC, keeping track of test systems could be handled through use of network discovery software. In addition to hardware, tools authorized for use on the network should be identified. It would also be appropriate to include a write-up of each tool in an appendix.

3.   Communication Strategy

3.1.   General Communication

Discusses frequency and methods of communication. For example, identify meeting schedule, locations, and conference call information if appropriate.

3.2.   Incident Handling and Response

This section is critical in the event that an incident occurs on the network while testing is in progress. Criteria for halting the information security testing should be provided, as should details on the test team's course of action in the event that a test procedure negatively impacts the network or an adversary attacks the organization while testing is underway. The organization's incident response call tree/chain of command should be provided in a quick-reference format. A process for reinstating the test team and resuming testing should also be provided.

4.   Target System/Network

Identifies the systems and/or networks to be tested throughout the information security testing process. Information should include authorized and unauthorized IP addresses or other distinguishing identifiers, if appropriate, for the systems (servers, workstations, firewalls, routers, etc.), operating systems, and any applications to be tested. It is also crucial to identify any system not authorized for testing—this is referred to as the "exclude list."

5.   Testing Execution

This section is specific to test type and scope, but should detail allowable and unallowable activities and include a description of the information security testing methodology. If necessary, an assessment plan should be developed that complements the ROE—this could be either an appendix or a separate document.

5.1.   Nontechnical Test Components

Identifies nontechnical test activities that will take place, and includes information to help identify the types of policies, procedures, and other documents that should be reviewed. If interviews or site surveys are to be conducted, guidelines should be established for advance approval of the interview list and questions. If physical security of information systems is in the scope of the testing, procedures should be determined and a form—with appropriate signatures and contact information—generated for the test team to show to law enforcement or onsite security personnel in the event that they are questioned.

5.2.   Technical Test Components

Includes the type of technical testing to be conducted (e.g., network scanning, discovery, penetration testing); discusses whether files are authorized to be installed, created, modified, and/or executed to facilitate testing; and explains the required actions for those files once testing is completed. Any additional information regarding the technical testing of the organization's systems and networks should also be included in this section. Significant detail should be included on what activities will occur on the target network to ensure that all parties are aware of what is authorized and to be expected as a result of the testing.

5.3.   Data Handling

Identifies guidelines for gathering, storing, transmitting, and destroying test data, and establishes detailed, unambiguous requirements for data handling. Keep in mind that data results from any type of information security test will identify vulnerabilities that an adversary can exploit, and should be considered sensitive.

6.   Reporting

Details reporting requirements and the report deliverables expected to be provided throughout the testing process and at its conclusion. Minimum information to be provided in each report (e.g., vulnerabilities and recommended mitigation techniques) and the frequency with which the reports will be delivered (e.g., daily status reports) should be included. A template may be provided as an appendix to the ROE to demonstrate report format and content.

7.   Signature Page

Designed to identify accountable parties and ensure that they know and understand their responsibilities throughout the testing process. At a minimum, the test team leader and the organization's senior management (CSO, CISO, CIO, etc.) should sign the ROE stating that they understand the test's scope and boundaries.

Appendix C—Application Security Testing and Examination

Application security testing and examination help an organization determine whether its custom application software—for example, Web applications—contains vulnerabilities that can be exploited, and whether the software behaves and interacts securely with its users, other applications (such as databases), and its execution environment. Application security can be assessed in a number of ways, ranging from source code review to penetration testing of the implemented application.[43] Many application security tests subject the application to known attack patterns typical for that application's type. These patterns may directly target the application itself, or may attempt to attack indirectly by targeting the execution environment or security infrastructure. Examples of attack patterns are information leakage (e.g., reconnaissance, exposure of sensitive information), authentication exploits, session management exploits, subversion (e.g., spoofing, impersonation, command injections), and denial of service attacks.

Application security assessment should be integrated into the software development life cycle of the application to ensure that it is performed throughout the life cycle. For example, code reviews can be performed as code is being implemented, rather than waiting until the entire application is ready for testing. Tests should also be performed periodically once an application has gone into production; when significant patches, updates, or other modifications are made; or when significant changes occur in the threat environment where the application operates.

Many application security testing and examination techniques are available. They can be divided into white box techniques, which involve direct analysis of the application's source code, and black box techniques, which are performed against the application's binary executable without source code knowledge.[44] Most assessments of custom applications are performed with white box techniques, since source code is usually available—however, these techniques cannot detect security defects in interfaces between components, nor can they identify security problems caused during compilation, linking, or installation-time configuration of the application. White box techniques still tend to be more efficient and cost-effective for finding security defects in custom applications than black box techniques. Black box techniques should be used primarily to assess the security of individual high-risk compiled components; interactions between components; and interactions between the entire application or application system with its users, other systems, and the external environment. Black box techniques should also be used to determine how effectively an application or application system can handle threats. Many tests use both white box and black box techniques—this combination is known as gray box testing.

Assessors performing application security assessments should have a certain baseline skill set. Guidelines for the minimum skill set include knowledge of specific programming languages and protocols; knowledge of application development and secure coding practices; understanding of the vulnerabilities introduced by poor coding practices; the ability to use automated software code review and other application security test tools; and knowledge of common application vulnerabilities.

---

[43] Some elements of application security testing, such as penetration testing an application, are target vulnerability validation techniques, not target identification and analysis techniques. Application security testing is discussed only in this section for brevity.

[44] Some applications, such as many web applications, do not have compiled (binary) executables, so black box techniques may not be applicable to analyzing their code.

Application security continues to grow in importance as attackers increasingly focus on application-layer attacks. Because application security assessment is a complex topic with dozens of commonly used techniques, it is outside the scope of this publication to provide specific information on techniques or recommendations for their use.[45] Appendix E provides references with additional information.

---

[45] In the future, NIST may release a separate publication on application security testing and examination.

TECHNICAL GUIDE TO INFORMATION SECURITY TESTING AND ASSESSMENT

Appendix D—Remote Access Testing

Remote access testing assesses remote access methods for vulnerabilities, and covers technologies such as terminal servers, VPNs, secure shell (SSH) tunnels, remote desktop applications, and dial-up modems. This testing is intended to discover alternative methods of entry into the network that circumvent perimeter defenses. Remote access testing is often conducted as part of penetration testing, but can also be performed separately to better focus on remote access implementations. Testing techniques vary according to the type of remote access being tested and the specific goals of the test. Examples of commonly used techniques include:

■ **Discovering unauthorized remote access services.** Port scanning may be used to locate open ports that are often associated with remote access services. Systems may be manually checked for remote access services by viewing running processes and installed applications.

■ **Reviewing rulesets to find unintended remote access paths.** Remote access rulesets, such as those on VPN gateways, should be reviewed for holes or misconfigurations that could permit unwanted access.

■ **Testing remote access authentication mechanisms.** Since remote access methods normally require authentication, testers should first verify that they are required to authenticate before they attempt to gain access. Testers can try default accounts and passwords (e.g., guest accounts, maintenance accounts) and brute-force attacks—and social engineering can also be used to attempt to get a password reset or to gain access without an authentication token (e.g., by claiming the token is lost). Testers can also attempt to gain access through self-service authentication programs that allow passwords to be reset by answering user-specific questions—this also may involve social engineering.

■ **Monitoring remote access communications.** Testers can monitor remote access communications with a network sniffer. If communications are not protected, testers may be able to use them as sources for remote access authentication information and other data sent and received by remote access users.

Active or intrusive remote access testing should be performed during times of low demand to limit potential disruption to employees and the remote access systems.

Another aspect of remote access testing is assessing an organization's phone systems for vulnerabilities that permit unauthorized or unsecured access. NIST SP 800-24, *PBX Vulnerability Analysis*[46], provides information on elements and approaches to private branch exchange (PBX) security testing. In the area of remote access, the primary target of phone system testing is modems—and although their use has decreased due to the wide availability of wired and wireless network access, successful attacks continue to be launched through unauthorized modems. For example, there are users who still use modems on their work computers for remote access, and some organizations use older technologies—such as building operations controllers and switches—that have maintenance modems enabled. A single compromise via a modem could allow an attacker direct, undetected access to a network that avoids perimeter security.

Several available software packages allow network administrators—and attackers—to dial large blocks of telephone numbers to search for available modems. This process is called *war dialing*. A computer with four modems can dial 10,000 numbers in a matter of days. War dialers provide reports on numbers with modems, and some dialers have the capacity to attempt limited automatic attacks when a modem is discovered. Organizations should conduct war dialing at least once per year to identify their unauthorized

---

[46] See http://csrc.nist.gov/publications/PubsSPs.html for additional information on PBX security.

modems, with testing conducted after normal business hours to limit potential disruption to employees and the organization's phone system. (It should be considered, however, that many unauthorized modems may be turned off after hours and might go undetected.) War dialing may also be used to detect fax equipment. Testing should include all numbers that belong to an organization, except those that could be impacted by receiving a large number of calls (e.g., 24-hour operation centers and emergency numbers).[47]

Skills needed to conduct remote access testing include TCP/IP and networking knowledge; knowledge of remote access technologies and protocols; knowledge of authentication and access control methods; general knowledge of telecommunications systems and modem/PBX operations; and the ability to use scanning and security testing tools such as war dialers.

---

[47] Most types of war dialing software allow testers to exempt specific numbers from the calling list.

Appendix E—Resources

This appendix lists a wide range of additional resources for use with technical security testing and examination. Table E-1 contains a list of NIST documents that complement this guide, and Table E-2 provides a list of online resources that organizations may reference for additional information.

Table E-1. Related NIST Documents[48]

NIST Document	URL
SP 800-30, *Risk Management Guide for Information Technology Systems*	http://csrc.nist.gov/publications/nistpubs/800-30/sp800-30.pdf
SP 800-40 Version 2.0, *Creating a Patch and Vulnerability Management Program*	http://csrc.nist.gov/publications/nistpubs/800-40-Ver2/SP800-40v2.pdf
SP 800-53 Revision 2, *Recommended Security Controls for Federal Information Systems*	http://csrc.nist.gov/publications/nistpubs/800-53-Rev2/sp800-53-rev2-final.pdf
SP 800-53A, *Guide for Assessing the Security Controls in Federal Information Systems*	http://csrc.nist.gov/publications/nistpubs/800-53A/SP800-53A-final-sz.pdf
SP 800-64 Revision 1, *Security Considerations in the Information System Development Life Cycle*	http://csrc.nist.gov/publications/nistpubs/800-64/NIST-SP800-64.pdf
SP 800-84, *Guide to Test, Training, and Exercise Programs for IT Plans and Capabilities*	http://csrc.nist.gov/publications/nistpubs/800-84/SP800-84.pdf
SP 800-92, *Guide to Computer Security Log Management*	http://csrc.nist.gov/publications/nistpubs/800-92/SP800-92.pdf
SP 800-94, *Guide to Intrusion Detection and Prevention Systems (IDPS)*	http://csrc.nist.gov/publications/nistpubs/800-94/SP800-94.pdf

Table E-2. Online Resources

Resource	URL
Methodologies	
Information Design Assurance Red Team (IDART)	http://www.idart.sandia.gov/
NIST SP 800-53A, *Guide for Assessing the Security Controls in Federal Information Systems*	http://csrc.nist.gov/publications/PubsSPs.html
National Security Agency (NSA) Information Assessment Methodology (IAM)	http://www.nsa.gov/ia/industry/education/iam.cfm?MenuID=10.2.4.2
Open Source Security Testing Methodology Manual (OSSTMM)	http://www.isecom.org/osstmm/
Open Web Application Security Project (OWASP) Testing Project	http://www.owasp.org/index.php/Category:OWASP_Testing_Project
Tools	
BackTrack (Linux live distribution)	http://www.remote-exploit.org/backtrack.html

---

[48] The base URL for all the NIST SPs is http://csrc.nist.gov/publications/PubsSPs.html.

Resource	URL
Extra – Knoppix (Linux live distribution)	http://www.knopper.net/knoppix-mirrors/index-en.html
F.I.R.E. (Linux live distribution)	http://fire.dmzs.com/
Helix (Linux live distribution)	http://www.e-fense.com/helix/
INSERT Rescue Security Toolkit (Linux live distribution)	http://www.inside-security.de/insert_en.html
Knoppix Security Tools Distribution (STD) (Linux live distribution)	http://s-t-d.org/download.html
nUbuntu (Linux live distribution)	http://www.nubuntu.org/downloads.php
Operator (Linux live distribution)	http://www.ussysadmin.com/operator/
PHLAK (Linux live distribution)	http://sourceforge.net/projects/phlakproject/
Top 100 Network Security Tools	http://sectools.org/
Vulnerability Information	
Common Configuration Enumeration (CCE)	http://cce.mitre.org/
Common Vulnerabilities and Exposures (CVE)	http://cve.mitre.org/
Common Weakness Enumeration (CWE)	http://cwe.mitre.org/
Default Password List	http://www.phenoelit-us.org/dpl/dpl.html
French Security Incident Response Team (FrSIRT)	http://www.frsirt.com/english/
iDefense Lab's Public Advisories List	http://labs.idefense.com/intelligence/vulnerabilities/
milw0rm	http://www.milw0rm.com/
National Vulnerability Database (NVD)	http://nvd.nist.gov/
Neohapsis Archives	http://archives.neohapsis.com/
Open Source Vulnerability Database	http://www.osvdb.org/
Open Web Application Security Project (OWASP) Vulnerabilities	http://www.owasp.org/index.php/Category:Vulnerability
Secunia Advisories	http://secunia.com/advisories/
SecurityFocus Vulnerabilities	http://www.securityfocus.com/vulnerabilities
SecurityTracker	http://www.securitytracker.com/
Secwatch's Vulnerability Archive	http://secwatch.org/advisories/
The Hacker's Choice (THC)	http://freeworld.thc.org/
United States Computer Emergency Readiness Team (US-CERT) Vulnerability Notes Database	http://www.kb.cert.org/vuls
Wireless Vulnerabilities and Exploits (WVE)	http://www.wirelessve.org/

Appendix F—Glossary

Selected terms used in the publication are defined below.

Active Security Testing: Security testing that involves direct interaction with a target, such as sending packets to a target.

Banner Grabbing: The process of capturing banner information—such as application type and version—that is transmitted by a remote port when a connection is initiated.

Covert Testing: Testing performed using covert methods and without the knowledge of the organization's IT staff, but with full knowledge and permission of upper management.

External Security Testing: Security testing conducted from outside the organization's security perimeter.

False Positive: An alert that incorrectly indicates that a vulnerability is present.

File Integrity Checking: Software that generates, stores, and compares message digests for files to detect changes made to the files.

Information Security Testing: The process of validating the effective implementation of security controls for information systems and networks, based on the organization's security requirements.

Internal Security Testing: Security testing conducted from inside the organization's security perimeter.

Network Discovery: The process of discovering active and responding hosts on a network, identifying weaknesses, and learning how the network operates.

Network Sniffing: A passive technique that monitors network communication, decodes protocols, and examines headers and payloads for information of interest. It is both a review technique and a target identification and analysis technique.

Operating System (OS) Fingerprinting: Analyzing characteristics of packets sent by a target, such as packet headers or listening ports, to identify the operating system in use on the target.

Overt Testing: Security testing performed with the knowledge and consent of the organization's IT staff.

Passive Security Testing: Security testing that does not involve any direct interaction with the targets, such as sending packets to a target.

Password Cracking: The process of recovering secret passwords stored in a computer system or transmitted over a network.

Penetration Testing: Security testing in which evaluators mimic real-world attacks in an attempt to identify ways to circumvent the security features of an application, system, or network. Penetration testing often involves issuing real attacks on real systems and data, using the same tools and techniques used by actual attackers. Most penetration tests involve looking for combinations of vulnerabilities on a single system or multiple systems that can be used to gain more access than could be achieved through a single vulnerability.

Phishing: A digital form of social engineering that uses authentic-looking—but bogus—e-mails to request information from users or direct them to a fake Web site that requests information.

Plan of Actions and Milestones (POA&M): A document that identifies tasks needing to be accomplished. It details resources required to accomplish the elements of the plan, any milestones for meeting the tasks, and scheduled milestone completion dates.

Port Scanner: A program that can remotely determine which ports on a system are open (e.g., whether systems allow connections through those ports).

Review Techniques: Passive information security testing techniques, generally conducted manually, that are used to evaluate systems, applications, networks, policies, and procedures to discover vulnerabilities. They include documentation, log, ruleset, and system configuration review; network sniffing; and file integrity checking.

Rogue Device: An unauthorized node on a network.

Rules of Engagement (ROE): Detailed guidelines and constraints regarding the execution of information security testing. The ROE is established before the start of a security test, and gives the test team authority to conduct defined activities without the need for additional permissions.

Ruleset: A collection of rules or signatures that network traffic or system activity is compared against to determine an action to take—such as forwarding or rejecting a packet, creating an alert, or allowing a system event.

Social Engineering: The process of attempting to trick someone into revealing information (e.g., a password).

Target Identification and Analysis Techniques: Information security testing techniques, mostly active and generally conducted using automated tools, that are used to identify systems, ports, services, and potential vulnerabilities. Target identification and analysis techniques include network discovery, network port and service identification, vulnerability scanning, wireless scanning, and application security testing.

Target Vulnerability Validation Techniques: Active information security testing techniques that corroborate the existence of vulnerabilities. They include password cracking, remote access testing, penetration testing, social engineering, and physical security testing.

Version Scanning: The process of identifying the service application and application version currently in use.

Virtual Machine (VM): Software that allows a single host to run one or more guest operating systems.

Vulnerability: Weakness in an information system, or in system security procedures, internal controls, or implementation, that could be exploited or triggered by a threat source.

Vulnerability Scanning: A technique used to identify hosts/host attributes and associated vulnerabilities.

Appendix G—Acronyms and Abbreviations

Selected acronyms and abbreviations used in this publication are defined below.

ARP	Address Resolution Protocol
ATA	Advanced Technology Attachment
C&A	Certification and Accreditation
CCE	Common Configuration Enumeration
CGE	Cisco Global Exploiter
CIO	Chief Information Officer
CIRT	Computer Incident Response Team
CISO	Chief Information Security Officer
CTO	Chief Technology Officer
CVE	Common Vulnerabilities and Exposures
CVSS	Common Vulnerability Scoring System
CWE	Common Weakness Enumeration
DNS	Domain Name System
DoS	Denial of Service
DSL	Digital Subscriber Line
FIPS	Federal Information Processing Standards
FISMA	Federal Information Security Management Act
FrSIRT	French Security Incident Response Team
FTP	File Transfer Protocol
GOTS	Government Off-the-Shelf
GPS	Global Positioning System
GUI	Graphical User Interface
HHS	Department of Health and Human Services
HTTP	Hypertext Transfer Protocol
IAM	Information Assessment Methodology
ICMP	Internet Control Message Protocol
IDART	Information Design Assurance Red Team
IDPS	Intrusion Detection and Prevention System
IDS	Intrusion Detection System
IEEE	Institute of Electrical and Electronics Engineers
IIS	Internet Information Server
IP	Internet Protocol
IPS	Intrusion Prevention System
ISSO	Information Systems Security Officer
IT	Information Technology
ITL	Information Technology Laboratory
LAN	Local Area Network
MAC	Media Access Control

NAT	Network Address Translation
NIS	Network Information System
NIST	National Institute of Standards and Technology
NSA	National Security Agency
NVD	National Vulnerability Database
OMB	Office of Management and Budget
OS	Operating System
OSSTMM	Open Source Security Testing Methodology Manual
OWASP	Open Web Application Security Project
P2P	Peer-to-Peer
PBX	Private Branch Exchange
PDA	Personal Digital Assistant
PII	Personally Identifiable Information
PIN	Personal Identification Number
POA&M	Plan of Action and Milestones
POP	Post Office Protocol
RF	Radio Frequency
ROE	Rules of Engagement
SCADA	Supervisory Control and Data Acquisition
SCAP	Security Content Automation Protocol
SHA	Secure Hash Algorithm
SIP	Session Initiation Protocol
SME	Subject Matter Expert
SMTP	Simple Mail Transfer Protocol
SP	Special Publication
SSH	Secure Shell
SSID	Service Set Identifier
SSL	Secure Sockets Layer
SSN	Social Security Number
STD	Security Tool Distribution
TCP	Transmission Control Protocol
TCP/IP	Transmission Control Protocol/Internet Protocol
TCP/UDP	Transmission Control Protocol/User Datagram Protocol
TFTP	Trivial File Transfer Protocol
THC	The Hacker's Choice
UDP	User Datagram Protocol
URL	Uniform Resource Locator
US-CERT	United States Computer Emergency Readiness Team
USB	Universal Serial Bus
VM	Virtual Machine
VoIP	Voice Over Internet Protocol
VPN	Virtual Private Network
WAN	Wide Area Network

WIDPS   Wireless Intrusion Detection and Prevention System
WLAN   Wireless Local Area Network
WVE   Wireless Vulnerabilities and Exploits

XML   Extensible Markup Language

www.ingramcontent.com/pod-product-compliance
Lightning Source LLC
Chambersburg PA
CBHW061628080326
40690CB00058B/4238